JESUS
CENTER OF CHRISTIANITY

BRENNAN R. HILL

ST. ANTHONY MESSENGER PRESS

Cincinnati, Ohio

To AUNTIE RIE and UNCLE GORDON (Marie and Gordon Bautz),

two exemplary disciples of the Lord. Their 70+ years of marriage

have been an inspiration to so many of authentic gospel love

and sacrifice for others.

Cover design and illustration by Constance Wolfer
Book design by Mary Alfieri
Electronic pagination and format design by Sandy L. Digman

ISBN 0-86716-367-4

Copyright ©2000, Brennan R. Hill

Published by St. Anthony Messenger Press
Printed in the U.S.A.

Contents

ACKNOWLEDGMENTS

Much gratitude to Jeremy Harrington, O.F.M., for inviting my wife, Marie, and me to produce the original twelve *Millennium Monthly* articles. Thanks also to Judy Ball for her excellent advice and editing of those articles. Special recognition to Bill Bruns and Lisa Biedenbach for their dedicated work on this expanded text.

Introduction

Many of these chapters first appeared as part of St. Anthony Messenger Press's answer to John Paul II's call to prepare for the opening of the new millennium. My wife, Marie, and I were privileged to prepare the *Millennium Monthly* for the first year, during which the theme was Jesus Christ. It was an exciting new project and received an overwhelming response, with more than 300,000 subscriptions. The wonderful reception generated the idea to gather these essays in one place in book form, with a number of new chapters added.

It is always a moving experience for me to write about Jesus. I wrote a book on the Master several years ago and will never forget what a mysterious experience it was. I had written other books, but they were about "topics." The book on Jesus was about a person, the very person who *is* at the heart of our Christian faith: the amazing individual who lived, died and was raised for us; the person whose Spirit now dwells in our hearts and our communities. I can remember in the midst of intense research getting new glimpses into his personality, his own faith struggle, indeed, into the extraordinary and unique character of this young Nazarene.

To write about Jesus is truly a graced experience. Such writing has brought me to realize more than ever before that Jesus was truly a human person, who lived in a specific time and place, and who had to struggle with the ups and downs of life just as the rest of us have to do. At times I have had sudden glimpses of him as I sat in library stalls, or as I read the insights of other scholars. He would often be a real presence for me in the faces of my students or in people with whom I discussed the chapter I was planning. Even the arduous process of putting this all into words on a computer screen, with Mozart playing in the background, was often a moment of contact and contemplation.

I have come to realize that the true center of Christianity is not a set of doctrines, a code of laws, a number of sacraments and rituals, church officials or such controversies as who should be ordained or which parishes should be closed. All of these have their importance, but the center of Christianity is a person—Jesus Christ. Without him, his life, teachings and risen presence among us, the other aspects of church life are without meaning and purpose. All discussion on Christian faith must begin and end with Jesus, the Son of God.

In these essays, I begin by returning to the center of things, Jesus Christ, the heart of Christian faith, who is the same yesterday, today and tomorrow. Then I turn to the past, to the historical Jesus. How I envy those who were privileged to know him. They could look into his dark, warm eyes, grasp his hand, listen to the lilt of his Aramaic tales, laugh with him, enjoy his table ministry and walk with him in the cool of the evening. We can only imagine, speculate, conjecture. And yet he was real, and, in the deep layers of the gospels, we can catch brief visions of this young Nazarene as he grows in wisdom and knowledge before the Lord, and as he goes from place to place plying his trade as a craftsman.

There are so many dimensions to this man from Galilee. The gospel images and stories reveal that Jesus was a faithful Jew, thoroughly committed to Torah, synagogue and Temple. We watch him as he listens for Abba's will, leaves his family and friends, and follows the call to be a preacher, teacher, healer and prophet. We listen as he beckons to the first disciples, a motley crew with little education and often with shady pasts. In an amazing departure from tradition, Jesus calls women to join his disciples, and prepares them to share his ministry and to hold key positions in the early communities.

Jesus was a man of prayer, whose experience of the Creator was unprecedented for its intimacy. He was a person of the desert, the mountain and the garden, where he opened his heart to the will of his Father. Jesus taught his followers to pray and urged them to see prayer as the fuel for compassionate and dedicated service to others.

Jesus was also a person who was free from the attachments that separate us from goodness and eternal life. He was free from sin, fear and possessions; from that grasping selfishness and greed that prevents so many from offering themselves to others. Therefore, Jesus was free to give, to reach out, to love, to sacrifice. Following him gives the same freedom to his disciples and provides them with the courage to step up against those who oppress people or degrade the earth.

Two of the sacramental symbols that Jesus gave us enable us to be one with him. In Baptism, the Son of God initiates us into his life and community. In Eucharist, the Lord nourishes our spirits, joins us more closely with other disciples, strengthens us with his risen presence and prepares us for his second coming.

We begin a new millennium as his disciples filled with hope for the Church, the people who make Christ's presence visible in the world. There is much to do as the world faces many new threats of nuclear destruction, chemical and germ warfare, increased violence, environmental crises, the breakdown of families and many other dangers. Paul once pointed out to the Christians in Rome, who were facing similar challenges, that they were groaning inwardly waiting for redemption and that indeed creation itself was "groaning in labor pains." Then Paul gave them reason for hope with these words: "For I am convinced that neither death, nor life, nor angels, nor rulers, nor things present, nor things to come, nor powers, nor height, nor depth, not anything else in all creation, will be able to separate us from the love of God in Christ Jesus our Lord" (Romans, 8:22-24; 38-39). For Paul and the early Christians, as well as for all Christians today, hope for the future is based on a central belief—Jesus is Lord!

CHAPTER ONE

The Center of Christianity Is a Person

Each Christmas I have always heard: "Jesus was born almost two thousand years ago." Well, the "almost" is now set aside with the celebration of the 2000th year since Jesus' birth. The opening of a new millennium is a profoundly significant event for those who proclaim along with the first disciples that "Jesus is Lord." We look back over two thousand years and commemorate the astounding occasion when our God "became one of us" in Jesus. We celebrate the time when the Spirit of the Lord began the Church. And we once again acknowledge that Jesus Christ, the risen Lord, is the center of Christianity.

Returning to Palestine

Recently, my wife, Marie, and I, along with thirteen friends, went on a pilgrimage to Israel. We were privileged to be able to visit the places where Jesus was born, grew up and worked as a craftsman. We swam in the lake where Jesus fished with his disciples, and walked the roads and hillsides where he preached and healed. We wept with tears of both sorrow and joy at the sites where he died and was raised.

Along the way, we would often remark, "He was actually *here*!" Even though we knew that Jesus could be experienced in any place, we seemed to encounter him in a unique fashion in his own land. We came to realize more than ever before that Jesus was a real flesh-and-blood person. Had we been privileged to live back in those days, we could have met him, looked into those mysterious dark eyes and enjoyed his friendship. We could have shared meals with him, laughed with him or sat on the rooftops in the cool of the evening to listen to his stories!

One occasion especially reminded me that it is the person of Jesus who is the center of Christianity. One morning, we joined several other groups on a boat for a trip across the Lake of Galilee. When we reached the center of the lake, the pilot stopped the motors and the group fell silent for some minutes. Then we began to read the gospel stories about this place. People from Italy, Latin America and the United States *were* on the boat. We had all traveled from afar to this lake on a sunny morning in honor of Jesus, our savior. I realized anew that without Jesus Christ, Christianity would have little meaning. Jesus is at the heart of Christian teaching and prayer, and yet how easy it can be to get distracted from this by lesser issues in our parishes or dioceses.

The Beginnings of Christianity

Christianity began when a young Jewish carpenter, Jesus of Nazareth, suddenly burst on the Galilean scene as a powerful teacher and gifted healer. Many in the crowds, and the special apostles and disciples whom Jesus handpicked, seemed to recognize that the power of the Lord God was acting through this young man. Early on, Jesus seemed to be trying to reform his own Jewish religion. Like the prophets of old, he called his people back to authentic Jewish living. "Repent," he proclaimed, "for the kingdom of heaven has come near" (Matthew 4:17b).

There seemed to be little room for a lukewarm response to Jesus of Nazareth. Either one accepted his teaching and repented, or one rejected Jesus as a false prophet. Many accepted Jesus and became part of his movement. Some simply walked away. Others felt threatened in their position and power by Jesus, and they decided to do away with him. We are familiar with the story. Jesus was arrested while at prayer, falsely accused, beaten and then executed naked outside the city on a cross. To Jesus' enemies, as well as to his followers, it must have appeared that the mission of this young preacher of God's love and forgiveness had come to a tragic end.

Resurrection Faith

But Jesus' death on the cross was not the end. Several days after Jesus' death, his faithful followers began to experience him as raised from the dead. The tomb had been found empty, and gradually the disciples encountered their Lord alive and glorified. They began to see that Jesus was the Son of God, their messiah and savior.

What had been a rag-tag group of shaky disciples now was suddenly galvanized into an inspired community witnessing to the good news of Jesus Christ. Peter would be transformed from an impetuous and even betraying person into a heroic apostle. He would stand before his fellow Jews, who had come to Jerusalem for the Hebrew Pentecost, and proclaim: "You that are Israelites, listen to what I have to say. Jesus of Nazareth, a man attested to you by God with deeds of power, wonders, and signs that God did through him among you, as you yourselves know—this man, handed over to you according to the definite plan and foreknowledge of God, you crucified and killed by the hands of those outside the law. But God raised him up..." (Acts 2:22-24). The fire of a "new" Pentecost had been ignited and would rapidly spread across the Roman Empire.

His Following Grows

Throughout the ages, countless numbers, beginning with Mary and the disciples, have accepted Jesus Christ as their savior, pledged themselves to live his gospel and received his promise of eternal life. There was Paul the Pharisee, who was on a mission to seek out and punish the Christians as "heretics." Paul was knocked down, struck blind and brought to realize that in persecuting Christians, he was indeed oppressing the risen Lord. Paul was taken to Damascus, where he himself accepted Jesus as the Christ. He spent the rest of his life spreading the gospel of Jesus and living in union with the

Lord. Thus he could write these touching words to the Galatians: "And it is no longer I who live, but it is Christ who lives in me" (Galatians 2:20).

Jesus would continue to move the hearts of many as time went on. At the turn of the first century, the well-loved bishop of Antioch, Ignatius, would be condemned by Rome for his faith in Jesus. He was ordered to Rome for execution by wild animals in the Colosseum. Along the way, Ignatius was met by other Christians, and his courage gave many of them strength to keep their faith. He cautioned those Roman Christians who wanted to risk their lives to save him not to interfere. His moving words to them echoed his love for Jesus in the Eucharist: "I am the wheat of God, and I must be ground by the teeth of wild beasts, so that I may become the pure bread of Christ" (Letter to the Romans 4,1).

This was the same Jesus who, many centuries later, inspired a young Italian, Francis, to give up the security of his home and set aside secular interests to have only one aim in his life: to love Christ and to imitate him as closely as he could. Francis died in 1226, and yet his spirit still fills his town of Assisi. During his life, Francis was looked upon as one who somehow was uniquely able to capture the spirit of his role model, Jesus. A prayer attributed to him is still treasured by many Christians: "Lord, make me an instrument of your peace...."

In the fifteenth century, the Spirit of Jesus would call a young French maiden to lead her country to victory over the English. She would see her king crowned in Rheims before her capture and condemnation as a "heretic." Young Joan would be burned at the stake, rather than give up her faith in the Lord. It is said that to the very end she held a cross and called out the name of Jesus, for he was the center of her faith.

Indeed, throughout the centuries, an incalculable number of people have followed the "narrow path" of Jesus, who has extended his invitation to women and men, rich and poor, saints and sinners, heroes and outcasts. Queens and serfs, nobles and paupers have heard his "Come, follow me" (Matthew 19:21), and have opened their hearts to forgiveness and new life. Each of them followed in the footsteps of the

Master who taught them the true purpose of life: "The Son of Man came not to be served but to serve and to give his life a ransom for many" (Matthew 20:28).

Jesus in Our Time

Many outstanding disciples of Jesus have lived in our own time. Dorothy Day, Thomas Merton and Archbishop Oscar Romero come to mind as people who have been symbols of Jesus' presence in our world. But Jesus also dwells in the hearts of many who lead hidden lives, lives that are often filled with suffering and sacrifice, love and compassion. Whether it be a parent forgiving a child, a young soldier offering a prayer before battle or a teen visiting a senior citizen, it is faith in Jesus that sustains Christians.

Many grieved to hear of the death in 1996 of Father Henri Nouwen, a Dutch priest and renowned spiritual writer who, in the end, discovered Jesus most vividly present in "the little ones." Father Nouwen's search for Jesus took him to widely diverse situations: from helping the mentally disturbed at the Menninger Clinic to teaching the best and the brightest at Harvard and Yale; from living with Trappist monks to working with peasant farmers in Latin America. Ultimately, he said, he found Jesus most vividly in the simple folk with mental and physical handicaps at a community in Canada known as L'Arche (the Ark).

At Nouwen's funeral, many of these "little ones" gathered around a homemade casket on which they had painted trees, the sun, rainbows and people. Slowly, they danced around the altar, gesturing to each others' hearts and to the coffin. They truly loved this priest, for he had touched their lives and helped them find Jesus in themselves. They remembered his words: "Jesus' appearance in our midst has made it clear that changing the human heart and changing human society are not separate tasks, but are as interconnected as the two beams of the cross."

At the opening of a new millennium, we celebrate the birth of Jesus as well as his presence and power in his people throughout the centuries. We pray that the Lord's invitation to follow him will be accepted by many generations to come, especially by our own children and grandchildren. As the letter to the Hebrews proclaimed: "Jesus Christ is the same yesterday and today and forever" (Hebrews 13:8).

For Reflection

- *Who or what is the center of your faith? Why?*

- *Describe your personal relationship with Jesus. How is it similar and different from your personal relationship with your spouse or best friend? How has your relationship with Jesus changed through the years—since you were a child, a teen, young adult and so on?*

- *What about Jesus attracts you? Which of his qualities or personality traits appeals to you so much that you want to follow him?*

- *Why do you think Jesus requires repentance of his followers? What do you require of the people who follow you?*

- *How do you preach the "good news" that Jesus preached?*

CHAPTER TWO

The Historical Jesus

Two thousand years is such a long time. It can make it difficult to remember that Jesus Christ really lived a human life at a particular period of history. But let's see if we can go back in time and see how life might have been for Jesus. Who were the people, what were the places that might have influenced him? What kind of a person was this Jesus of Nazareth?

The Nazarene

If you had been alive in those days, it would have been possible for you to have actually seen Jesus in Nazareth, a small Jewish village in northern Palestine. You could perhaps have been his neighbor, or even a relative. I have always envied those fortunate people who had personal contact with Jesus. They watched him play in the streets and worked side by side with him during the harvests.

Some saw him helping his mother Mary bring the heavy water jugs from the well or working on a project with his father, Joseph. Others sat with him in synagogue school, where Jesus received a simple education in the rudiments of Jewish life. There were those who traveled with him in the long caravans to Jerusalem to celebrate the great Jewish feasts.

A Rugged Workman

Surely Jesus' appearance was different from what we usually see in much religious art. Jesus was a Mediterranean Jew, a "country person" from the Middle East. He was no doubt dark-featured, and his skin would have been deeply tanned and weathered. Jesus worked with his hands as a carpenter for most of his life. He probably built some of the houses in his neighborhood, provided furniture for needy folks and most likely worked on construction sites in cities nearby.

Jesus would not have been a willowy figure in a snowy white robe, but a rugged and muscular carpenter. I often compare Jesus to the young workmen who come to my campus to repair and renovate our buildings. When they stand next to me in the cafeteria, their hands are rough and calloused, their faces weathered and their physiques toughened and muscular from hard work. When I see them, I often think to myself: "That is how Jesus must have looked."

Unique Neighbor

Some of Jesus' neighbors in Nazareth no doubt realized early on that this young man was close to God. Those who heard him speak of God as *Abba* (Dad), must have wondered how he could be so familiar with the Creator. Other villagers must have seen that Jesus was a man of prayer, a person of deep compassion and love. He was the kind of person who would show up when people were in need. From the beginning, Jesus must have shown a special affection for children, the sick and those who lived on the margins of life. His friends must have been at times amazed at his deep faith and his insights into the Scriptures. What memorable evenings they must have spent with him after a hard day's work, sitting at table and sharing food and conversation with him!

Not everyone in Nazareth liked Jesus. Once he began his public ministry, some apparently thought he was "uppity" and too filled with ambitions that seemed prophet-like, even messianic. Luke tells a story of one of Jesus' homecomings after preaching in the synagogues of Galilee. Jesus attended the Sabbath synagogue service and was asked to be a "lector." He read from the prophet Isaiah: "The Spirit of the Lord is upon me, because he has anointed me to bring good news to the poor. He has sent me to proclaim release to the captives and recovery of sight to the blind...." At the end of the reading, Jesus did the unexpected. He looked directly at the members of the congregation and said, "Today this Scripture has been fulfilled in your hearing" (see Luke 4:14-30).

Some of Jesus' old neighbors were so furious with the "nerve" of this lowly "son of Joseph" that they drove him out of town and tried to throw him off a cliff. Jesus later commented on his disappointment in his hometown neighbors and relatives: "Prophets are not without honor except in their own country and in their own house" (Matthew 13:57).

Jesus the Galilean

Jesus grew up, worked and preached in the northern province of Palestine, which was called Galilee. Jews had lived in this area for thousands of years and had often been victims of conquests. About fifty years before Jesus' birth, Palestine had been invaded by the Roman legions and incorporated into the Empire. Many of Jesus' fellow Jewish Galileans had lost their land and homes to Roman loyalists. These disenfranchised Jews worked as poor tenant farmers, tradesmen and struggling fishermen. Most resented the domination and oppression that they had to endure. One might compare their feelings to those of many Irish or Palestinians today.

The Galileans were known to be rugged country types who lived close to the land. When we hear the simple parables of Jesus about harvests, fruit trees, flowers and the birds of the air, his Galilean background is apparent. When we listen to his stories about farmers sowing their seeds and shepherds protecting their sheep, we hear echoes of Jesus' youth on the hillsides of Galilee.

Galileans were also known for their independent and rebellious natures. In the past, they had rejected tyrannical leaders like Herod and his family. Several times during Jesus' childhood, violent rebellions were mounted by Galilean Jews. Jesus no doubt carried childhood memories of soldiers retaliating by burning towns to the ground and selling Jews into slavery. Along the hillsides of Galilee, he may have seen horrible crucifixions of those considered to be dangerous to Rome. He knew early on that this could happen to him if he took a stand against injustice or oppression. When Jesus' time did come, it would be a Herod who mocked him and handed him over to be crucified.

Jesus no doubt also objected to the oppression of the Roman leadership, especially the brutal procurator Pilate. The Gospel of Luke tells us that Pilate once murdered some of Jesus' fellow Galileans while they were devoutly offering sacrifice to their God (Luke 13:1). Pilate would have been incensed by Jesus' remark to give Caesar only the coin of taxation and not the tribute of worship that the Romans thought Caesar deserved. He would have been outraged that Jesus drove the merchants and money-changers from the Temple, for Rome shared heavily in their profits. We recall how it was Pilate who had Jesus mocked and scourged, and who gave permission for him to be crucified.

As a Galilean, Jesus was never bitter, hateful or violent toward those who oppressed him and his people. He taught forgiveness and love of enemies, blessed peacemakers, and preached mercy and compassion. While he condemned hypocrisy and reproached those who put "heavy burdens" on the poor and oppressed "outcasts," Jesus was not a violent man. One need only look at Luke's account of the crucifixion. The young Jesus had been unjustly condemned and nailed naked to a cross. His life slowly ebbed from his body with every tortured breath. Yet no curses or condemnations were heard from his lips. Jesus simply said, "Father, forgive them for they do not know what they are doing." Then he turned to the condemned criminal at his side and promised him, "[T]oday you will be with me in Paradise" (Luke 23:34,43).

Our Parents Shape Our Lives

Jewish mothers, even today, can have profound influence on their sons. Mary, the mother of Jesus, was an extraordinary woman. The gospel stories about her indicate strong memories of her deep faith, prophetic power, compassion and courage. As a young teen, she was asked to consent to conceive a son by the power of the Spirit. Her answer was simply, "Be it done unto me." When she went to help Elizabeth, Mary's words were far beyond her age.

Her Magnificat proclaims the greatness of God and predicts the uplifting of the lowly and the downfall of the high and mighty. Memories of Mary's compassion for others and her confidence in her son come through in the story of the first miracle at Cana. Her courage and fidelity are recalled in the accounts of her vigil at the foot of her son's cross.

We can indeed see the reflections of Mary's influence in the life of her son, Jesus. He seems to have learned from her how to turn his life over to God. "Not my will but thine be done," he said, in the garden the evening of his arrest. Mary seems to have taught her son well to stand with the downtrodden, reach out to the oppressed and confront the unjust. Her compassion was passed on to her son and comes through often in his healing miracles and acts of forgiveness. On Calvary their courage and fidelity became one. Jesus dies giving his mother to all: "Behold thy mother."

'I Am Joseph, Your Brother'

Jesus' foster father, Joseph, was also an outstanding person. The gospel stories about him echo memories of his hard work, forgiveness, faith and courage. Joseph's young bride-to-be had apparently become pregnant by another man, so he initially decided to divorce her quietly rather than publicly humiliate her. When Joseph heard the miraculous explanation of Mary's pregnancy, he accepted it and married Mary without question. In the story of the Magi, Joseph is portrayed as courageously taking his family into Egypt to protect them from Herod's savagery.

Jesus learned much from Joseph. He worked most of his life at the trade that his father taught him. Jesus seems to have learned well lessons of forgiveness from Joseph. He was known to forgive even the most rejected sinner with a simple word. These lessons in courage carried Jesus through threats and rejection and even through an excruciating death on a cross.

In November 1996, we witnessed the passing of one of Joseph's namesakes, Cardinal Joseph Bernardin. He came before his many friends with the greeting that was heard by Jacob's brothers in ancient Egypt, in Jesus' neighborhood, in the welcomings of Pope John XXIII and in Chicago: "I am Joseph, your brother."

The cardinal, who showed us not only how to live like Jesus but also how to die like him, told a story of his own father. One day his dad had just come home from cancer-related surgery on his left shoulder, which was heavily bandaged under his white shirt. Suddenly his son, little Joseph, fell backwards over a railing and began crying. With no thought to his own condition, the father jumped the railing and gathered his little boy in his arms. The cardinal remembered seeing the blood soaking through his father's shirt. He said that he was always deeply touched by his father's spirit of self-sacrifice, a gift he obviously embodied himself. The spirit of Joseph that so affected Jesus and many others lives on!

Yes, Jesus of Nazareth lived two thousand years ago in ancient Nazareth of Galilee. Like us, he was shaped by the places and people of his time. Even though Jesus now lives in our midst as the risen Lord and Savior, it is helpful to visualize him as a person in his own milieu. The historical Jesus can help us better appreciate our own human potential and teach us to live our lives fully with dignity and virtue.

For Reflection

- *Many of Jesus' neighbors rejected him and his teachings because he was just "the boy next door." When have you failed to recognize God in those you know well? How do you feel when people fail to recognize God in you?*

- *Think of your favorite image, painting or drawing of Jesus. Why is it your favorite?*

- *At the wedding reception at Cana, Mary told the wine steward, "Do whatever he tells you." When have you done whatever Jesus tells you? Can you list three important things that Jesus has told his followers to do?*

- *Why is it important to come to know Jesus as a real human being who lived at a certain time in history and in a specific culture?*

- *A national religious publication sponsored a contest for artists to create a new image of Jesus for the new millennium—using any medium. What would your contest entry be?*

CHAPTER THREE

Jesus, Faithful Jew

I have always known that some people had a certain prejudice against Jews, but I never realized how savage anti-Semitism could be until I met Rujik, a Hungarian seminarian. At the time I was an undergraduate at St. Bonaventure University, and Rujik was in an art class with me. One day after lunch he invited me to his room to look at some of his sketches. We sat down at a table and Rujik opened a large album and began turning the pages. I was shocked at what I saw. On each page there was a Jewish figure being brutalized in some fashion. Some were being stabbed, while others were being beaten, shot, tortured, or hung. Rujik saw my shock and said: "These people are the Christ-killers and this is what they deserve." As he explained how such hatred of Jews was common in his country, I began to realize how the Holocaust had come to pass in Europe during the 1940's.

I will never forget that day when I saw those sketches. How ironic! Here was a young man studying to be a priest who would preach Jesus Christ, and yet he despised the very people to whom Jesus belonged, the Jews. Did Rujik not realize that Jesus himself was a faithful follower of the Hebrew religion and that Judaism is the very foundation of Christian Scriptures and belief?

Jesus the Jew

We often forget that Jesus was a real human individual, a person of flesh and blood raised by Jewish parents in a small Jewish enclave called Nazareth. From his childhood, Jesus had been told the stories of the Hebrew Scriptures and had been taught to follow the beliefs and laws of Torah. Jesus followed the commandments of Moses, led his life according to the prescriptions of his people, and prayed the Psalms and other Hebrew prayers. He no doubt attended the tiny synagogue in his area, where he received instructions and listened to the readings of Scripture. From time to time, Jesus would accompany his family and relatives on the long trip up to Jerusalem to celebrate the great feasts in the Temple. Jesus earned his living as a craftsman who always honored the Sabbath; he preached as a teacher who was trying to renew his own religion; and he died as a religious reformer whose teachings were considered to be dangerous by many of his own religious leaders. In short, one cannot understand Jesus without knowing his people, the Jews.

Jesus, of course, was a Jew who was shaped by the places where he lived and by the various types of people around him. Earlier we discussed how growing up in Nazareth with his parents, Mary and Joseph, helped form Jesus' personality. In this chapter, we will look at Jesus in the context of Palestinian Judaism of his time, specifically comparing and contrasting him to some of the contemporary religious figures of his day.

A Jew of Palestine

Jesus grew up in an ancient area of the world known since five hundred years before his time as Palestine. (Present-day Israel is a part of Palestine.) Jesus' people had lived there for thousands of years, since the days of the patriarchs Abraham, Isaac and Jacob. Jesus' Hebrew ancestors were a people who had seen the glory days when their nation flourished under kings like Saul, David and Solomon. But they had also been conquered and dominated by the great powers of Babylon, Persia, Greece and Rome. Through it all, the Hebrews were called to remain a chosen people who believed in the one God, Yahweh.

The Romans had conquered Jesus' area about fifty years before he was born. The Romans quickly confiscated the lush coastal lands and pushed the Jewish population into the hinterlands, where many of them were forced to eke out their existence. Jesus knew well the brutal oppression of the Roman soldiers, the greedy threats of the tax-collectors and the tyranny of the Herodian family who served as puppet leaders for the Romans. He watched as his neighbors were sold into slavery for not paying their heavy land mortgages or taxes. He listened to stories by the night fires of relatives who had been beaten to death or crucified for criticizing the harsh policies of the government. Jesus was no doubt warned by his elders that if he stepped out of line and challenged the powers that be, his punishment would be swift and brutal.

The Essenes

The Essenes were a religious group prevalent in Jesus' times and study of them can help us better understand his identity. Modern interest in this group started in 1947, when many of their scrolls were discovered in Qumran, near the Dead Sea. It is estimated that thousands of Essenes lived in communities throughout Israel in Jesus' day, and hundreds dwelt in the monastery at Qumran. Jesus would have seen these ascetical white-robed monks moving from monastery to monastery, and no doubt would have felt a certain kinship with them. The Essenes were devout, sectarian Jews who valued community, prayer and shared meals. They were ardent in their messianic expectations, and many of them believed that the end of the world was imminent. Like Jesus, the Essenes warned of the power of Satan and preached the righteousness of the poor as opposed to the corruption of the rich. They anticipated that their great leader, whom they called the Teacher of Righteousness, would be persecuted.

Though parallels exist between Jesus and the Essenes, and there are even possible influences by them on the later Christian communities, there are also striking contrasts. The Essene version of Judaism denied the validity of the Temple and the priesthood in Jerusalem. Instead, the Essenes saw themselves as the "chosen ones." Salvation would come only to those who joined them, a largely male, celibate community that rigidly followed a set of complex rules. They were a highly clerical group with a strict hierarchical structure. They were purists, who allowed neither cripples, the blind, nor those with any other disabilities to belong. These desert monks taught hatred of the rich and of any enemy, and rejection of the unclean and sinful.

The contrasts between Jesus and the Essenes are obvious. Jesus was orthodox in his acceptance of the Temple and the priesthood in Jerusalem. His understanding of the Jews being "chosen ones" was much more inclusive than that of the Essenes. Jesus taught of an Abba God who was both the creator and the savior of all creation. Jesus' prayer was for oneness, not division; and his gospel would be for "all nations," not a select few. Jesus included all in his discipleship and healing ministry: women, men, rich, poor, the healthy as well as the disabled. Jesus did not require celibacy of his apostles or disciples, and he taught that authority was to be humble service rather than oppressive domination. Jesus taught love of the enemy and of the unclean and sinful. He urged his disciples to be compassionate and forgiving, not self-righteous and judgmental. These were ancient Hebrew values, and Jesus was dedicated to restoring them to his people.

The Zealots

It is unlikely that there was a well-organized party of Zealots in Jesus' times, but there were movements of Jewish terrorists working to drive Rome out of their land and to punish all those who collaborated with the enemy occupiers. Some of these were mere thugs and hoodlums, but others were ardent and devout patriots filled with the zeal of the Lord to liberate their people. For them, force and terrorism seemed to be the only way to open the way to God's kingdom. They believed that they were allied with a God of vengeance who would bring judgment and death to all the enemies of the Creator. Theirs was a holy war of vengeance and wrath toward all their enemies.

Again, there must have been common ground between

Jesus and the Zealots. After all, at least one of the apostles was probably a Zealot or a former member of that sect. Jesus, of course, would have been in sympathy with the Zealot's indignation over Roman domination and oppression. He too prayed that the kingdom would come, and he wanted freedom for his people. Yet, Jesus had no part with hatred of enemies, nor with violence. He taught his disciples to turn the other cheek in courageous and passive resistance. He told them to love their enemies and to pray for those who persecuted them. The Master advocated forgiveness seventy times seven and brought peace to his disciples. Even in the midst of his own unjust and treacherous crucifixion, Jesus prayed for forgiveness for his executors. As a dedicated Jew, Jesus was "zealous" for the Lord, but it was with the zeal of a peacemaker and an advocate, not with that of an assassin or an avenger.

The Sadducees

Of all the groups of Jews in the Palestine of Jesus' time, the Sadducees stood most in contrast to Jesus of Nazareth. The Sadducees were the aristocrats of the time. They included the chief priests and noblemen, who controlled the Temple and the Sanhedrin in Jerusalem and owned most of the land throughout Judea and Galilee. As recent excavations under the Temple mount in Jerusalem show, the Sadducees lived sumptuous lives. At the same time, they were conservative guardians of the laws of the written tradition and punished severely anyone who disobeyed the law or rebelled against their authority. Their power was usually paid for through their support of the Roman occupation and by their willingness to share the enormous income from the Temple celebrations with imperial leaders.

It is easy to see why the Sadducees would react so strongly to Jesus and play a central role in his execution. He was, of course, neither from the priestly nor aristocratic classes. Rather, Jesus was of peasant stock, a young man from a poor rural background who had made a living with his hands. Jesus had strong words of criticism for hypocrites, the greedy rich, and those who laid the heavy burdens of legalism on the backs of the poor. And, of course, many of the Sadducees fit those descriptions rather well.

Jesus was indeed an observant Jew, and yet he saw love as the highest law and was willing to bend the law when it came to helping others or standing up for outcasts. The gospels show us how enraged the Jewish leaders became when Jesus healed on the Sabbath or associated with those who they considered "unclean." The fact that Jesus befriended sinners, fraternized with the disabled and actually called women to be his disciples would have appalled the Sadducees. They no doubt saw Jesus as a dangerous upstart who was, in fact, challenging their authority with his behavior and with his teachings on afterlife, divine providence and prophetic expectation of the messiah.

The Scribes

One would think that Jesus would compare well with the scribes of his time since, like them, he was a strong leader and a dedicated teacher. But here, too, there were striking differences. The scribes were the highly educated theologians and canon lawyers of the time who had spent many years at the feet of a master in one of the exclusive schools in Jerusalem. During their years of schooling, they would act as servants to their teacher as they learned the many scholarly opinions on Jewish written and oral tradition. The scribes were held in high esteem, and when they went out in the public, they were followed by crowds who clamored to hear their teaching. When the scribes showed up in the synagogue or at Temple feasts, they expected to be given the highest places of honor.

Jesus, of course, though a learned teacher, never attended any of the fine schools in Jerusalem. His learning would have come through the tiny synagogue school in Nazareth or from his informal discussions with his neighbors after a hard day's work. Jesus had no formal credentials to teach the way he did. Moreover, he did not choose his disciples from the rich intelligentsia the way the scribes did. Rather, Jesus chose both rich and poor, often illiterate common folk, women and men, and people with shady reputations because they were or had been Zealots or tax collectors.

Never did Jesus consider his followers to be his servants. Instead he told them that he was their friend and that if they wished to be first, they would have to be last. Furthermore, Jesus offered an example of meekness and humility and never expected the places of honor. And when he taught, generally he told down-to-earth stories that the masses could understand and apply to their lives. Jesus did not delve into scholarly interpretations of the law or the intricacies of theological debate.

The Pharisees

Of all the religious figures of his time, Jesus seems to have had the most in common with the Pharisees. That might be surprising to many since the Pharisees generally have the reputation for being rigid legalists and even self-righteous hypocrites. (Many scholars tell us that this negative image of the Pharisees comes from a time long after Jesus when the Gospels were being written and Christians were being persecuted by Pharisees.)

Actually, the Pharisees of Jesus' day were usually identified with the common folk and often toiled as "social workers" among the poor. They were open to both written and oral law and were generally flexible interpreters of the law because they were dealing with the real life of ordinary people. The Pharisees generally opposed cooperation with their Roman conquerors, but they did not approve of the violent opposition used by the Zealots. They gathered in communities, valued table fellowship and lived a simple life-style. Many of the Pharisees of Jesus' time preached the need for conversion of heart and taught that acts of love and justice were more important than ritual observance.

One can see many similarities between Jesus and the Pharisees. Still there are differences in that Jesus uniquely spoke of God as Abba, the loving parent, and opened his table ministry to the most rejected sinners and outcasts. Jesus spoke of a healing God and thus challenged the more common pharisaical view that God punishes through disease and disability. Jesus was much more flexible about legal observance than most of the Pharisees. He opened salvation to all, and his teachings on forgiveness and freedom went far beyond that of the Pharisees.

Devout and Faithful Jew

We have seen that Jesus was indeed a devout and faithful Jew. His mission in life was to reform and renew his own religion and not to start a new one. As a Palestinian Jew of his time, he was shaped by the events and the culture around him. Jesus' life and mission can be seen as having similarities and differences with the other religious figures of his time. All this points up that Jesus, even though unique in his teaching and living of Judaism, was indeed thoroughly Jewish. Thus, there is no room in Christianity for anti-Semitism. Indeed Christians should look at Judaism as the very root from which Jesus and Christianity grew, respect Judaism as its own heritage and see Jews as their spiritual sisters and brothers.

For Reflection

- *In its Declaration on the Relations of the Church to Non-Christian Religions* (Nostra Aetate), *the Second Vatican Council definitively taught that "neither all Jews indiscriminately at that time [of Jesus] nor Jews today, can be charged with the crime committed during his [Jesus'] passion...Jews should not be spoken of as rejected or accursed as if this followed from holy Scripture" (#4). How do you feel when you hear anti-Semitic statements or witness anti-Semitic behavior?*

- *It's often easy to blame the Nazis for anti-Semitism in our time. However, others (members of the Ku Klux Klan, various "skin-head" groups and perhaps even a neighbor or coworker) are also guilty of this sin. As a Catholic Christian, what do you do to counteract anti-Semitism?*

- *Can you think of any modern groups that are similar to the*

Zealots? the Pharisees? the Sadducees? the Essenes? the scribes? In what ways are they similar? In what ways do they differ?

- *As a disciple of Jesus, how are you inclusive in your words and actions? Have you ever been excluded because of your race, age, sex, nationality or religious belief? If yes, how did you feel and how did you respond?*

CHAPTER FOUR

Jesus, Teacher and Prophet

No teacher has influenced so many people as Jesus of Nazareth. Countless numbers have heard his gospel message and uprooted their lives to follow him. Jesus' challenge to "[S]ell what you own, and give the money to the poor" (Mark 10:21) drew followers like Francis of Assisi and Mother Teresa of Calcutta to live simply and give of themselves, serving the poorest of the poor. His message, "I am the way, and the truth, and the life" (John 14:6) moved Thomas Aquinas and Teresa of Avila to dedicate themselves to lives of study and prayer. Jesus' teaching that his disciples should turn the other cheek when someone abused them (Luke 6:29) drew people such as Mohandas Gandhi, Dorothy Day, Martin Luther King, Jr., and Desmond Tutu to lead nonviolent protests against injustice. Multitudes of people have placed their hopes for meaning here and eternal life hereafter in "the Master."

Surely most of us can remember special verses from the gospels that changed our lives and helped us through hard times. My mother's favorite passage was: "[H]er sins, which were many, have been forgiven; hence she has shown great love" (Luke 7:47). When she was dying, those words helped her overcome her fears and have a peaceful death.

Teacher Among Teachers

Jesus can become more real for us when we see him in the context of his times. Many teachers in his day taught lessons similar to those of the preacher from Nazareth. The ascetical Cynics preached that riches did not bring happiness and that worry about such matters as clothes and food could only bring anxiety. Rabbi Shammai's teachings on divorce were very controversial. The people of Jesus' time dearly loved Rabbi Hillel, who served the poor and taught them self-respect. Hillel, like Jesus, taught his disciples to treat others as they would want to be treated. The many learned scribes explained Torah and used parables to interpret the laws of God. Another great teacher, John the Baptist, called sinners to repentance and preached that the kingdom of God was at hand. Though similar to these other teachers, Jesus of Nazareth stands as unique and incomparable.

Jesus was such a striking teacher that many people could not understand how he had learned so much while working as a carpenter in tiny Nazareth. On one occasion when Jesus returned there to teach in the synagogue, his former neighbors were astonished at his teachings. After all, Jesus had never studied under a famous scribe in one of the elite rabbinical schools in Jerusalem. Like other Nazarenes, Jesus had studied in the small village school until he was twelve. Weekly, he would have listened to the readings of Torah and the Prophets and prayed with his fellow villagers in their synagogue. No doubt some of Jesus' friends and relatives remembered gathering with him on his rooftop after a hard day's work to discuss their beliefs. But they never expected to hear him teach with such power and authority!

Teacher With Unique Credentials

Some of those who were close to Jesus probably did have some idea of how he became such a great teacher. Mary no doubt remembered sharing with him her own deep faith, concerns about helping the poor in the village and strong determination to be faithful to God. She recalled how Jesus had learned from Joseph to be hard-working and honest in his trade. Joseph also had much to teach Jesus about forgiveness, dedication and humility. We know little of Mary and Joseph really, but their lives are reflected in their son, Jesus.

Although Jesus did not have the official credentials of a learned scribe, a scholarly Essene or a Pharisee highly practiced

in the law, he had learned by "drinking from his own well."
Jesus had gleaned profound lessons firsthand from his family,
his life of deep prayer and his close attention to the movement
of the Spirit. The inspiration possibly came on caravan trips to
Jerusalem, where Jesus was moved by the magnificence of the
Temple and yet shocked at the corruption he saw in the city. Or
the revelations might have come when Jesus was about the
tasks of his trade, concerned about serving others with his
skilled carpenter's hands. Possibly the insights came on Jesus'
trips to mountaintops to pray, or during the time he spent in
prayer and fasting in the harsh wilderness of the desert.

Jesus experienced a profound intimacy with his God, and
called him "Abba" (gentle and loving dad). Jesus knew in ways
not accessible to any person the presence and power of this
ever-creating, forgiving and loving God. For Jesus, this gracious
God was at hand and able to be known intimately in nature,
children, the poor and outcasts. He came to realize that the
kingdom of God that had been spoken of in the Scriptures was
not a kingdom of domination, violence, greed or hatred. God's
reign was one of love, justice, forgiveness and healing.

Jesus' faith in God, himself and his world all seemed to
come together when he was baptized by John. Jesus saw again
that he was loved by his Father and was now called to bring the
good news to others. As Jesus came from the water, he heard,
"You are my Son, the Beloved; with you I am well pleased"
(Luke 3:22). He would make one last retreat in the desert and
begin his public life as a teacher.

A Call to Conversion

Jesus taught that, in order to be open to Abba's loving and
saving presence, people must repent. Repentance means to
retrace one's steps, to change direction. It means to radically
change from focusing on self to centering on God and neighbor.
Jesus called his followers to give up their sinful ways. He told
tax collectors to avoid greed and dishonesty; he charged
soldiers to give up violence and fraud. Jesus told religious
leaders to stop putting heavy burdens on the backs of their

people. He told people to love their enemies.

For many, the call to discipleship meant radically changing their lives by leaving their trades or even their families. Jesus even asked one young rich man to give all that he had to the poor. One would have to pay dearly to follow the Master. Jesus calls for sacrifice, at times even the offering of one's life.

Although Jesus seems to have had a mission to reform his own Jewish religion, he reached out beyond his own people to Romans, Syro-Phoenicians, the hated Samaritans, indeed "all nations." Jesus had learned from Abba that all people are children of God and that God's saving mercy and love were for all to enjoy. This alone was a hard saying for those who felt that they belonged to the "chosen" people. But Jesus went even further. He included outcasts and the most rejected sinners in God's love and mercy. He startled the rich and famous by proclaiming, "Blessed are the poor" (Luke 6:20).

Jesus went out of his way to include everyone in his friendship. His "table" ministry included tax collectors, rebels, prostitutes and non-Jews. Many thought Jesus was carrying much too far his teaching on the inclusive love of Abba. Even Jesus' own relatives began to think that he had lost his mind. His enemies spread the word that Jesus was a glutton, drunkard and a friend of sinners. Some said he was doing the work of Satan. Yet, Jesus never backed away from his teaching, even when it became clear that it was going to cost him his life.

One of Jesus' most singular decisions was to extend his teaching to women. This was rare in the Judaism of Jesus' time. Women usually were thought too inferior to learn Torah and were considered too unclean even to sit in the main section of Temple or synagogue for prayers and readings. When women appeared in public they were to be fully covered and silent. Ignoring these restrictions, Jesus both taught and healed women in public. Stories of Jesus working his first miracle for his mother, of Mary of Bethany learning at Jesus' feet at her home, of the women at Calvary and the tomb all indicate that women were integral to the teaching and discipleship of Jesus.

A Prophetic Teacher

When Jesus began his teaching, his people had not seen a prophet for nearly four hundred years. When this Galilean burst on the scene, he caused the kind of amazement that had not been seen since the time of Zechariah and Malachi. At one point, Jesus' disciples told him that some people even thought that he was one of the ancient prophets.

The prophets were generally a tough-minded and outspoken lot. They believed that they were speaking in the name of God as they stood up to corrupt kings and rulers and cried out against injustice and oppression. The prophets were not primarily predictors of the future. Rather, they were conveyors of God's word and bearers of warnings of how God was going to punish evildoers. In their teachings, they would often use the so-called apocalyptic approach. This "end of the world" theme arose during times of crisis for the Jews. At such times, the Jews would cry out for God's help, and the prophets would predict that ultimately God would crush their enemies and save his people.

Jesus at times associated himself with the Hebrew prophets. After his reading of Isaiah in the synagogue at Nazareth, he told the people there that he was identifying himself with Isaiah's mission of liberation. He once pointed out that prophets aren't accepted by their own people, and on other occasions alluded to his own death by observing how prophets were often killed because of their views. Jesus sounded most like a prophet when he condemned religious leaders for hypocrisy and self-righteousness, calling them snakes, blind fools and tombs filled with bones. Jesus was perhaps most prophetic when he spoke up for the defenseless, the "little ones" of the world.

Jesus and the End of the World

As the new millennium approaches, there is much talk about the so-called "end of the world." Many people in Jesus' day also spoke of the endtime, and imagined that God would soon come with his heavenly armies, defeat their enemies and restore Israel. *Apocalypse* is the Greek word for *revelation*. The Bible contains a number of highly symbolic revelations on how God will come to defeat the forces of evil. The Book of Daniel portrays such a battle with evil in the Hebrew Scriptures, and the Book of Revelation does the same in the New Testament. Taking any of these stories too literally can be dangerous. Recall the tragic end David Koresh brought upon his Branch Davidians. Koresh was convinced that he knew when the end of the world would come and, ironically, brought about a fiery "apocalyptic" ending for himself and his unfortunate followers.

Jesus himself at times used apocalyptic images. In Mark's Gospel, he warned about the destruction of the Temple, told of the "signs" to look for, and warned that the end is coming. Jesus did admit, however, that even he did not know when the end would come. He simply said, "Watch."

In Matthew's Gospel, there is also "the last judgment," when the Son of Man separates the sheep and the goats and the king gives out just rewards and punishments. While Jesus occasionally used such ominous Hebrew images, in his own life he stressed mercy and forgiveness. He favored the image of a shepherd going out to look for the lost sheep over that of a judge sending sinners to everlasting fire.

Jesus' disciples look toward a new creation, a time of fulfillment and completion. We believe that God's love and goodness are stronger forces than evil and will prevail. We enter a new millennium in hope rather than in fear. Jesus *will* come again: today, tomorrow and at the end. We "stand fast" because our "redemption is drawing near" (Luke 21:28).

For Reflection

- *Did you have a teacher or coach or scoutmaster or some other adult who greatly influenced you and the path your life took? What was the effect that this person had on you?*

- *What Scripture passage speaks to you the most? Why?*

- *Jesus related to God as "Abba" or "Dad." What name would you give to your relationship with God? Why?*

- *Many theologians believe that all sin is rooted in idolatry because the sinner has substituted someone or something for God in his or her life. When have you substituted "idols" for God?*

- *How do you read the Book of Revelation—as a message of hope or a prediction of doom?*

CHAPTER FIVE

Jesus Calls Us to Be Disciples

I find myself at times struggling with the questions, "What is God calling me to do, and am I doing it?" I was told when I was young that God put each of us here for a reason. Identifying the reason is not always easy. Many of us continue to search for our calling, never quite sure if we've got it right.

Discipleship is about calling. It is about Jesus uniquely calling each of us to follow him. When we read the earliest Christians' writings, which still bear the memories of those who knew Jesus, we see people who had a deep affection for him and who found happiness in imitating his life. Answering Jesus' call to "Follow me" (Mark 1:17) has helped many better deal with that haunting question, "What am I supposed to be doing with my life?"

A Call to Repentance

Jesus began his call to discipleship with a simple but profound challenge: "Repent, for the kingdom of heaven has come near" (Matthew 4:17). Repentance means to turn around, retrace our steps and go in the right direction. Repentance is a call to "root out" the evil from our hearts and come home to God.

Jesus indicated why such a change of heart was needed and how to effect this change when he said "the kingdom of heaven has come near." In other words, God's loving and saving presence is within us and our world. We cannot convert our own hearts without help. Only the Spirit's presence and power can reveal who we really are and what we should be doing with our lives.

In Jesus' time, this call for conversion was difficult for many of his listeners. Just as now, there were those who thought they already had it made. Many of the wealthy and powerful Sadducees felt they had found their calling and were being rewarded with luxurious estates on the hillsides of Jerusalem. The learned scribes generally prided themselves on having answers to all the complex questions about the law. They expected preference for their superior wisdom and behavior. These figures were among those whom Jesus described as the "self-righteous." They were people who believed that righteousness or holiness could be self-achieved, without need for the grace of God. Jesus could be harsh on these types, calling them "hypocrites," "blind guides" and even "tombs filled with bones."

By contrast, there were many people then, just as now, who never thought they had a chance to make it at all. These were the vast numbers of poor tenant farmers, slaves, beggars and prostitutes. Many were physically or mentally ill; others were outcasts who believed that God was punishing them through these afflictions. Other people were caught up in sin and so filled with guilt and despair that they appeared to be possessed. Many of them had drifted as far from their true calling as had the proud and greedy.

Jesus Shakes the Foundations

When Jesus began to preach, it must have seemed that an earthquake had hit Palestine. He shook the very foundations of the Jewish tradition of his time. He said the poor were the blessed ones, the last would be first, and the meek would inherit the earth. Jesus gave special attention to the "little ones." He raised up those who had despaired that their lives had no purpose. Jesus blessed and healed those who thought they had been cursed by God with sickness and deformity. He became friends with helpless children and with women who had been abused or tossed aside by writs of divorce. He forgave those who were so caught up in evil that they had given up hope of mercy. To all of them he extended a call to the self-esteem, dignity and genuine self-love that is due a child of God.

Those who had been confident they were following God's calling were often challenged by Jesus. He showed the rich how their wealth could prevent them from being with God. Jesus criticized those dedicated to "mammon," and scoffed at their huge storage barns and buried treasures. He told one rich young man who wanted to be a disciple that he would have to give all his wealth to the poor. The young man sadly declined.

To follow Jesus, one would have to let go of attachments to things, share with others and put more effort in giving than in getting. This is not to say that Jesus condemned people with money or authority. Remember that he counted among his friends Joseph of Arimathea, a rich man of high rank who handed over his own tomb so that Jesus could be buried with dignity. Nicodemus the Pharisee and some of the scribes were also followers of Jesus, as well as a Roman commander. Mary Magdalene (who, by the way, is never described as a prostitute in the Gospels) apparently was a woman of independent means who helped support Jesus' ministry. Joanna, who was one of the first to hear of Jesus' resurrection, was the wife of the minister of finance in Herod's court. All these people had found their calling by listening to Jesus and applying his teaching and example to their own everyday lives. He helped them find the best within themselves with three simple words: "Come, follow me." Jesus would now be "the way and the truth and the life" (John 14:6).

A Call to Faith

When we read the gospel stories, we see that people were often amazed at Jesus' teachings and his miracles. Yet, Jesus was not looking for amazement; he was looking for faith. He wanted his disciples to join him in his saving mission and never turn back. In fact, the few times that Jesus is portrayed in the Gospels as angry or impatient are when people lacked genuine faith. The Gospel of Mark tells the story of a great storm on the

Sea of Galilee and how the disciples panicked. Even after the storm was calmed by Jesus, the disciples were still afraid. One can almost hear the frustration in Jesus' voice as he asks them, "Have you still no faith?" (Mark 4:40). Mark tells the story of another storm where Jesus actually walked to them on the sea to save his disciples. Yet, all he could get from them was astonishment because "their hearts were hardened" (Mark 6:52).

The kind of faith that Jesus called for in his followers was a deep and abiding trust in him as friend and teacher. Matthew gives an example of this kind of faith in the story of the two blind men who noisily came running after Jesus, asking for his pity. Jesus looked at them squarely and said, "Do you believe that I am able to do this?" With no hesitation the two blind men replied, "Yes, Lord." Jesus touched their eyes and said, "According to your faith, let it be done to you" (Matthew 9:27-29). The men received their sight from the Lord and forever stand as examples of that risk-taking, breathless, pursuing kind of faith that Jesus wants of his disciples.

Jesus, Man of Faith

We often forget that Jesus himself was a man of faith. He was truly human and therefore had to put his life in the hands of God. Jesus listened in prayer for what his Father was asking him to do.

Remember that he spent most of his life working at his trade, waiting for the inner call to leave home and become a preacher and healer. There may have been times when his mother, Mary, wondered why he was taking so long to decide what he was going to do with his life. And once he did finally start on his mission and she saw how dangerous it was, perhaps she wondered whether he ever should have left the security of his home and trade.

The Gospel of Mark tells of one afternoon when Jesus must have had a difficult time discerning what the Father was asking of him. First, Jesus was asked by Jairus to hurry and heal his dying daughter, and immediately Jesus headed off. On the way, Jesus' cloak was touched by a woman who hoped to be cured of hemorrhaging. Now Jesus knew that curing a woman of such an affliction in public would render him unclean and bring serious criticism from his enemies. He could have continued on his way to Jairus' house, but instead he stopped, commended the woman for her faith and healed her.

The delay kept him from healing Jairus' daughter, and Jesus was told that she had died. Still, Jesus did not waver in his faith. He told the grieving Jairus to have faith, and then revived the girl. Jesus then returned to Nazareth and was amazed that his own people were so lacking in faith that he could cure only a few of them. When the whole trip ended, Jesus must have reflected at length about what he was being called to do (Mark 5:21-43; 6:1-6).

We also find Jesus searching for his Father's will in the garden before his arrest. He felt dread at the prospect of crucifixion and prayed that, if possible, he would not have to go through with it. At the same time his faith moved him to place himself in the Father's hands. If God willed that he continue his mission even to death, then so be it.

The Gospels of Mark and Matthew make it clear that Jesus also was struggling to understand God's will at the very end. From the cross Jesus cried out in abandonment, "My God, my God, why have you forsaken me?" (Mark 15:34). Yet Luke assures us that even in his horrible crucifixion, Jesus never lost his trust in the Father. In this Gospel, Jesus died saying, "Father, into your hands I commend my spirit" (Luke 23:46).

A Call to Service

Discipleship also calls us to serve others. It calls a mother or father to get up in the middle of the night to care for a sick child; it calls a physician to make efforts to relax a nervous patient before an operation. It moves a trucker to stop his rig to help a motorist in distress, or a clerk to help an elderly person with her grocery bags. Discipleship is a way of life.

We are awakening to the realization that faith is also concerned about justice—for people, for all living things and for the earth itself. It is faith in the Lord that moves Michael, one of my students, to work four days a week providing healthy diets for the homeless. It is faith that stirs one of my neighbors to leave the security and comfort of her suburban home several days a week to bring the homeless to health clinics and dentists. Some of us may even be called to sacrifice our lives in the cause of justice. Regularly we hear of disciples in places like Rwanda, Algeria or Sudan being killed for taking a stand with the oppressed.

This is a crucial time to reflect on discipleship; a moment in history when all of us Christians might examine just how faithfully we have responded to the Lord's call to repentance, faith and service of others.

For Reflection

- *The words "discipleship," "disciple" and "discipline" all share the same Latin root, discere, which means "to learn." How does a Christian best learn about the discipline needed to become a true disciple of Jesus? What disciplines do you practice?*

- *When have you experienced a clear call from God? Did you respond to the call? If you haven't heard such a call, do you expect one? Should you?*

- *Jesus' teaching, especially in his parables, turned the world upside down. When has your world been turned upside down? How do you respond to surprises?*

- *When has someone asked you to "get out of the boat" and do something uncharacteristic or which required risk on your part? What did you do?*

- *How does the old saying, "Don't just do something, sit there!" apply to discipleship?*

CHAPTER SIX

Jesus and Women

I recently returned from leading a group of pilgrims to retrace the footsteps of Saint Paul in Greece. As we moved from Philippi to Berea, Thessilonica, Corinth and Athens, we reflected on the mission of this great apostle, prayed over his writings and searched for remnants of these ancient Christian communities.

We were struck by many things on this journey: Paul's physical endurance to withstand the heat and long walks on foot through lands that were often dangerous; his tenacity to withstand hostility, imprisonment, and all kinds of rejection and suffering in order to preach Jesus crucified. We also became more deeply aware of the important role that women had in Paul's mission.

It is indeed somewhat surprising that Paul the Apostle was so open to recognize a woman like Phoebe as a leader of an early community; to listen seriously to Chloe's report on the difficulties in the Corinth community; to acknowledge the valuable missionary activity of Priscilla in Rome and Corinth; and to give special recognition to such important women as Lydia, Tryphosa, Olympas and Junia.

Paul's openness to women playing important roles in the Christian communities was not typical of someone brought up in a patriarchal Jewish culture who studied the strict rabbinic teachings in Jerusalem. As a Pharisee, Paul learned that wives were property and that women were to stay in the background in religion. Some of those beliefs come through in Paul's letter when he tells women to cover their heads and be silent in church. But when Paul gets down to the heart of Christian belief he writes: "There is no longer Jew or Greek, there is no longer slave or free, there is no longer male or female; for all of you are one in Christ Jesus" (Galatians 3:28). He told all the members of his fledgling Churches, both women and men: "For freedom Christ has set us free. Stand firm, therefore, and do not submit again to a yoke of slavery" (Galatians 5:1).

Paul's pharisaical background could not have provided him with such liberal views. He must have learned of such equality from his Christian mentors in Antioch and elsewhere after his conversion. These Christian teachers carefully instructed him with Jesus' own words: "So if the Son makes you free, you will be free indeed" (John 8:36). Early on, Paul learned that all Jesus' followers were sisters and brothers and that all shared in the Lord's ministry. In the communities of the new testament, women were to be free and equal members of Jesus' Churches. This unique, indeed revolutionary, position toward women had been evident in the life and teachings of the Master himself.

The Gender Debate in Galilee

Growing up, Jesus would have heard his fellow Jews often debating issues about gender. We can only speculate on his thoughts on these matters during the synagogue teachings or when his neighbors and friends discussed these matters on the rooftops in the cool of the evening. Jesus knew well that there were two creation stories: a very early one which viewed woman as an appendage to man, created to be his helper. He no doubt engaged in the discussions concerning the meaning of the story that depicts Eve believing the serpent over God and how her decision to eat of the fruit and persuade Adam to do the same ruined their happiness and helped bring evil into the world.

Jesus would have also known about a later and more sophisticated creation story in which a cosmic God creates all with a simple word and then crowns the process by making humans, both male and female, in the divine likeness. This story, more than the Adam and Eve story, seems to have deeply influenced Jesus' later attitudes toward women and perhaps enabled him to challenge the oppression of women that he saw around him.

Patriarchal Structures

Jesus' belief that both females and males were created in the image and likeness of God and his deep love for all God's children moved him to oppose many of the abuses of women in the Jewish society of his time. Jesus' deep commitment to love, compassion and forgiveness stood in stark contrast to the unjust divorce laws that permitted men to throw their wives out for reasons so trivial as their poor cooking or their physical appearance. Jesus' respect for the dignity of all persons, especially outcasts, contradicted practices where daughters could be sold by their fathers, or where women could be punished for talking to a man in public. No doubt he found it absurd that women could not be taught Torah or assume places of honor in Temple. Jesus made it clear that women would be given equal respect in his community. Among his disciples, women would be taught the gospel message along with the men and would share in ministry.

Friend to Outcasts

In many of the gospel stories, Jesus is portrayed as ignoring the Jewish prejudicial practices toward women of that time. He freely speaks to women in public and treats them with respect, even when they are outcasts. The author of Mark's Gospel tells a touching story of a woman who had been hemorrhaging for twelve years and had spent all her money on physicians, with no results. Desperate, she risked public disgrace by appearing in the streets, and she touched Jesus' robe hoping for a cure. Jesus showed no fear of being considered "unclean" by having any dealings with her. Rather, he addressed her as though she were a child of his own: "Daughter, your faith has made you well; go in peace, and be healed of your disease" (Mark 5:21-34).

The Gospel of Luke tells another story of a rejected woman who comes uninvited to an all-male dinner at the house of Simon the Pharisee. She was probably a prostitute and "had some nerve" crashing the dinner at all. Coming to Jesus as a servant, she washes and kisses his feet, and then dries them with her hair. The guests were indignant and no doubt smirked to themselves at this unlikely relationship. Jesus, on the other hand, was not embarrassed in the least. He raised her up before the group as a woman filled with faith and love, and even commented how her hospitality was much more impressive than that of his host, Simon (Luke 7:36-50). Such a scene must have been unparalleled in the lives of these Pharisees!

And then there is the well-known story in John's Gospel of the woman caught in adultery. (The woman has been publicly humiliated and is about to be stoned. There is no mention of punishment for her male partner!) Jesus calmly steps into this highly volatile and dangerous situation and says: "Let anyone among you who is without sin be the first to throw a stone at her" (John 8:7). The religious leaders silently leave the scene one by one, no doubt embarrassed and angry, resolved to one day get even with this young, arrogant preacher. Jesus, in turn, kindly tells the woman that he does not judge her and that she is now free to go her way and not sin again.

Calling Women Disciples

Jesus' calling of women disciples was unprecedented in the Jewish religion of his time. The scribal schools were for men only; the communities of Pharisees were exclusive; and there were no women members to be found among the Sadducees, in most of the Essene communities, or among the teachers of the time. While it is true that Jesus chose males to be his apostles, the varying lists of these men in the Gospels seem to be more symbolic of the twelve tribes of Israel than having to do with gender issues. We know little of the ministry of the apostles, and as they died they were not replaced, with the exception of Judas' successor, Matthias. Although the apostolic witness was of enormous value, it is clear that Jesus was also accompanied by women disciples. These same disciples were prominently with Jesus during his crucifixion and were indeed the first witnesses to his resurrection.

Some Key Women Disciples

The Gospels tell us of a number of key women disciples who played significant roles in Jesus' life and mission. The women in these gospel stories are not only based on memories of women disciples, they also symbolize the integral role which women played in the later communities that produced the Gospels.

First and foremost is Mary, the mother of Jesus. In Luke's account of the nativity of Jesus, the incarnation itself awaits the consent of the young maiden, Mary (Luke 1:26-38). Mary is portrayed as the "Lord's servant," the central image for discipleship in the early Christian communities. In her Magnificat, she speaks like a young teacher and prophetess on her share in God's mission to the oppressed and the poor. In the story when the twelve-year-old Jesus is lost, Mary meets the challenge of her young son and returns him home for eighteen more years of nurturing and preparation (Luke 2:42-52). At Cana, Mary again waves aside the rebuke of her young son and has her way as she prepares the way for his first miracle (John 2:1-12). Here Mary becomes a partner in Jesus' ministry and at the same time symbolizes the sacramental role that women played in the Johannine community.

At Calvary, Mary is at Jesus' side and through her son's words is made partners in ministry with the Beloved Disciple. Mary was also part of the pentecostal community that received the Spirit and began shaping the Church. Moreover, Mary has stood through the ages as the epitome of faithful discipleship and can certainly be a role model for women today who wish to achieve equality and freedom in the Church.

Mary Magdalene, a woman of independent means, helped support Jesus' mission and was one of his closest disciples. There is, of course, no indication whatsoever in the Gospels that Mary Magdalene had ever been a prostitute or that she was in love with Jesus. These notions are the fantasies of modern movie producers and novelists. The gospel stories instead portray Mary as a key disciple, loyally with Jesus even to the end at Calvary. Moreover, she is the first to witness the Lord risen, and is commissioned by Jesus to spread the word to others (John 20:17). It is no wonder that in the early Church writings Mary Magdalene is referred to as an "apostle to the apostles." Mary can indeed be an effective symbol of the stature women can and should have in today's Church.

The two sisters, Martha and Mary, are also examples of the place women disciples played in Jesus' life. Jesus probably stayed with them and their brother Lazarus when he pilgrimaged to Jerusalem. In the gospel stories Jesus teaches them his message in their home. Martha plays a central role in the resuscitation of her brother Lazarus and receives the revelation of resurrection from Jesus himself. Mary is a contemplative listener of Jesus' word and at a miniature "last supper" anoints the feet of Jesus with her best perfume and dries them with her hair. Both sisters are striking symbols of how closely women can be associated with Jesus and his mission.

And, of course, there were others: the Samaritan woman at the well, whom Jesus converts and sends to be his witness to her town. There is Joanna, who left the luxury of Herod's court to live the simple life with Jesus. She, too, is portrayed as one of the original witnesses to the resurrection, and was sent to bring the good news to the disciples.

The Scriptures portray these women and others as missionaries, teachers, prophets, preachers, apostles, healers and leaders of house Churches. These women were pioneers in ministry and should serve as exemplars for the many women disciples today who feel called to share in Jesus' ministry.

Refocus on Jesus' Attitude Toward Women

One of the most painful struggles in Catholicism today is that of women who wish to gain equality in the Church. Today Church authority and official ministry are still almost exclusively in the hands of male priests and the hierarchy.

Many talented and well-trained women find it impossible to follow their "calling" in such a Church. I have known a number of outstanding and deeply spiritual women who have felt called to ministry, even to the priesthood. Tragically, many of them have moved to the periphery of the Church or even have simply left to serve elsewhere because they did not find acceptance in the official ministry of the Church. What a shameful loss to the spreading of Jesus' teaching and the carrying on of his ministry!

In my view, one way to help bring women to equality in the Church is to refocus on Jesus' attitude toward women and to study how Jesus' teachings played out in the earliest Christian communities. We must constantly return to our Scriptures, pay heed to our biblical scholars, listen to the pleas of women disciples today and search for an answer to this crucial question regarding women's place in today's Church.

For Reflection

- *How is or isn't your local parish or congregation inclusive of any and all people who want to be a part of it? What do you do intentionally in your faith community and as an individual to make people—even the marginalized—feel welcome?*

- *It is a custom since apostolic times for Christians to refer to each other as "sister" or "brother," especially in religious orders of men and women. How do you treat people as sisters and brothers?*

- *In rejecting the move to ordain women to the priesthood, Pope John Paul II and others have said that the Church is not empowered to make such a change because it has never been in our tradition because Jesus intentionally chose males as his apostles. How do you feel about this situation and the Church's teaching about it?*

CHAPTER SEVEN

Jesus, Man of Prayer

M y Aunt Helen died not long ago. My wife, Marie, our son, B.J., and I were at her bedside just before the end, recalling old times and praying with her. When we left, Helen smiled and blew us kisses as though she knew she was going home to the Lord.

Remembrance of Helen is a good place to start this reflection on Jesus and prayer, because it was she who taught me how to pray. My mother and I moved in with her when my father left us. It was Helen who opened a five-year-old's heart to the faith and taught him prayer. I remember asking her, "Who taught you how to pray?" She replied simply, "Jesus."

Model of Prayer

Prayer is often described as talking with God. Who better, then, to teach us prayer than Jesus, who shared every moment of his life with his loving parent, Abba? Who better to teach us than the Son of God himself?

We know that gospel stories were written by the early Christian disciples. These ancient stories with all their symbols reveal much about the prayer of Jesus. They can also teach a great deal about what prayer meant to the early Christian communities.

Throughout the Gospels we often find Jesus at prayer. There are scenes of high drama where Jesus prays at his baptism or on a mountaintop. There are quiet times when Jesus prayed alone at sunrise. Some are the formal prayers of synagogue, while others are quiet and compassionate words over those who needed forgiveness or healing. There are Jesus' magnificent prayers at his Last Supper, his poignant plea in the garden, and his prayers of agony, forgiveness and acceptance on the cross. All these stories of the Master's prayers can also help us with our own efforts to commune with God. Let's examine three of these gospel stories.

Prayer at the River

Jesus' baptism was a turning point in his life. Thus far he had worked quietly as a carpenter. Stepping into the river Jordan signified that Jesus would now be "plunged" into a new life. Jesus would have to leave his mother and the security of his home and go down a new and dangerous road. He would now have to confront evil openly and call sinners to repentance.

Luke's Gospel tells us that Jesus prayed at his baptism and then recounts a scene during Jesus' prayer that echoes one of the creation stories in Genesis. Creation seemed to be starting all over again with the Spirit hovering over the water and the Creator speaking from the heavens. In the midst of contemplation, Jesus heard, "You are my Son, the Beloved; with you I am well pleased" (Luke 3:22). Jesus now seemed to have a deeper self-awareness and went to the desert to listen for God's call. After his mentor, John, was executed, Jesus stepped up and began his own work as a healer and teacher.

Thomas Merton, a key spiritual writer of the twentieth century, often taught that prayer requires moving away from the "exterior self" toward the "inner self." The exterior self consists of the roles we play and the superficial identities that others give us. The inner self is the self as it came from God's creative hand, the self that is made in the likeness of God. This is the self wherein God dwells and waits to meet us in graced and prayerful contemplation.

Merton often wrote about how difficult it was to find this inner self. He describes his own self as a "shy and wild animal" who lived deep within and could only be drawn out when it was quiet and peaceful. Prayer is encountering God within and beyond this authentic self. Merton writes, "If we enter into ourselves, find the true self, and then pass beyond the inner 'I,' we sail forth into the immense darkness in which we confront the 'I am' of the Almighty. Our inmost 'I' exists in God and God dwells in it."

Jesus' prayer at his baptism was no doubt an experience of such intimacy with his Abba. Like all of us, Jesus also would have struggled with his self-image. Yet all along, Jesus surely knew that he was more than a good Jewish boy, a bright student, or a skilled carpenter. Jesus must have experienced an inner self that was uniquely one with God. Later, in his Last Supper prayer, Jesus would say that he and the Father were one. Now at his baptism, Jesus received a profound affirmation that he was indeed the beloved Son of God.

The prayer of Jesus at the river teaches us to look for God deep within our inner selves. Jesus teaches us that prayer nourishes humility, truthfulness and honesty about ourselves. Jesus calls us to a prayer that is simple and open, a prayer that regularly listens for the voice of God to affirm who we are and who we are called to be. Prayer is a time to listen to God's loving voice within. It is an opportunity to realize that we people of all colors, creeds, and nationalities are children of God.

Prayer in the Desert

On our recent pilgrimage to the Holy Land, we saw the wilderness where Jesus experienced his temptations. From a hillside overlooking Jericho, we could look up at this vast and stark expanse of rocky desert. Jesus must have been a hardy and courageous person to stay there by himself for forty days!

For the Jews, the desert was a symbol of liberation. It is the place where God cared for and fed them, forgave them their sins and led them to the promised land. The desert can make one feel weak and vulnerable. In the desert, Jesus experienced loneliness, danger and deprivation. His fasting from food and water intensified his discomfort. In the midst of all this, came his temptations to be false to himself. In the gospel account, the devil tempted Jesus to perform magic, amazing stunts and even devil worship. For these, he was promised wealth and power.

Jesus conquered these temptations and turned to God for the courage he would need to begin his ministry to others.

Jesus' desert prayer teaches us to look for solitude where we can honestly face—and even accept—our dark, shadowy side. It calls us to quietly repent of the ways we have hurt ourselves or others. Prayer also can be a source of strength to overcome the many temptations we face.

We all have our deserts, the barren stretches of life where there seems to be little meaning: the dry spells where even God appears to have abandoned us. Prayer is sometimes just waiting and listening for the Lord. It is the breathing and heartbeat of the spiritual life. In prayer, each of us can hear our unique call to ministry and receive the courage to answer.

In the desert, Jesus told the devil that people cannot live by bread alone but need the words of God. I have found that the "living word" of Scripture can be most helpful in prayer. Prayer with the Scriptures can provide authentic "daily bread" and indeed feed us with the "Bread of Life" himself.

Prayer on a Mountain

Mountains also have symbolic value in the Scriptures. It was on a mountain that Abraham was tested by God and that Moses received the Law. The mountains of Galilee are where Jesus commonly went aside to pray and where he often preached.

The Gospels tell a story of Jesus taking three of his apostles to the solitude of a mountaintop. Jesus had just come from Caesarea Philippi, which still today is a marvelous little oasis with cool running water. At this oasis, Jesus seemed to be struggling with his own identity, for he asked his disciples who they and others thought he was. Jesus was possibly anxious about the suffering and death ahead. He was angry with Peter and called him "Satan" for his not wanting Jesus to die. This was a foreboding Jesus who warned his disciples about the crosses they would have to carry and challenged them to "lose" their lives if they wished to be saved (Luke 9:28-29).

Jesus brought all these concerns to the mountaintop and

entered deeply into prayer. He prayed with such intensity that his whole appearance was transfigured. When the apostles saw him this way they were excited and wanted to put up three tents and stay there. As at Jesus' baptism, a voice came from the heavens. But now the voice addressed the disciples, "This is my Son, my Chosen; listen to him" (Luke 9:35).

Jesus' mountain prayer teaches us that we can seek comfort and refuge in prayer. In times when we are confused about just who we are or what we should be doing, prayer can enlighten and give direction. Prayer can help raise us from depression or discouragement. It can help us deal with the death of a loved one. Prayer can help restore confidence and hope if we have lost a job or have been betrayed by a friend. Prayer can also be a time to celebrate happy times and successes with our family or friends.

Sometimes only prayer can enable us to forgive an enemy and move beyond hatred and resentment. Martin Luther King, Jr., said that on occasions when he was beaten, called names by the police and thrown in jail, the only thing that saved him from bitterness was prayer. Filled with anger, he would kneel down and pray for those who had just abused him. Dr. King said that every time he did this his peace of mind would return and he would hold no grudges against his enemies.

Prayer can transfigure us. We can bring our dreams and our hopes, our self-doubts and fears to the mountaintop. We can leave our alienation and bitterness behind and come down filled with the good news that we are beloved children of God.

Cardinal Bernardin on Prayer

I have mentioned Cardinal Bernardin several times in this book. I suppose I must have him on my mind and see him as a saint of our times. In *The Gift of Peace*, the wonderful little book he wrote before his death, the cardinal tells a revealing story about his own prayer life. One evening he invited three young priests to dinner. During their conversation he told them that he was finding it difficult to pray and asked them if they could help. The young priests were surprised at then-Archbishop

Bernardin's request and candidly told him that a bishop shouldn't be urging others to pray when he himself wasn't giving enough time to prayer. They advised him to give real quality time to prayer.

The cardinal writes that after that conversation he decided to give God the first hour of each day for prayer. He describes the whole process as a "letting go" of everything that keeps "the Lord from finding hospitality in my soul or interferes with my surrender to what God asks of me." He writes that this decision to open each day with an hour of prayer put his life in a new and uplifting perspective. It was prayer that gave him the strength to face false charges and deadly cancer with forgiveness and faith.

I close with two prayers. The first is the prayer that one of Jesus' disciples said just as Jesus had finished meditating: "Lord, teach us how to pray" (Luke 11:1). The other one is for my Aunt Helen, who passed on to me the Lord's lessons on prayer: May she rest in peace.

For Reflection

- *How and when did you learn to pray?*

- *What form of prayer appeals to you most—meditation, memorized prayers, the rosary or other devotions, the Jesus Prayer, Centering Prayer, Lectio Divina, the Mass, Liturgy of the Hours? Why? How do you make prayer part of your daily routine?*

- *What benefits do you receive from prayer? What surprises you about prayer?*

- *When has God answered your prayer of petition? Do you believe that God answers all prayers of petition? Why or why not?*

- *Would you describe your prayer life as mostly talking to God or as mostly listening to God? What are the benefits of each?*

CHAPTER EIGHT

Jesus and Service to the World

It is time again in our parish to form a new catechumenate—another gathering of people who wish to become disciples of Jesus in our Church. What a privilege it was last Easter to meet with those who had just become Catholics! Their faces shone with joy and peace. Their hearts seemed to be filled with love. I understood more clearly Paul's words to the Galatians that "the fruit of the Spirit is love, joy, peace, patience, kindness, generosity, faithfulness, gentleness, and self-control" (Galatians 5:22-23). After two thousand years, the Spirit of the Lord is still with us as he promised.

Mindy, an attractive young wife and mother, came with a bouquet and a gift basket for Sister Marie, our parish director who had so carefully led us through this yearlong journey of conversion. Mindy glowed with happiness and said that since her entrance into the Church she has wanted to reach out to others in love and be a more giving person than she had been in the past. Mindy witnessed to what following Jesus is all about—being of service to others.

Learning in Nazareth

When we meet Jesus in the Gospels, he is a loving and generous adult who is most willing to give of himself to people in need. I have often wondered how he came to be such a caring person. How did he develop the ability to be able to reach out to so many different kinds of people with such openness and kindness? When did he discover that, with a mere touch or a word, God's healing power would come from him? At what point did Jesus realize that he was called to sacrifice himself for others?

Nazareth was a Jewish ghetto in Galilee, the northern province of Palestine. Many of Jesus' neighbors had been displaced by the Romans and worked as poor tenant farmers or shepherds for wealthy landowners in Jerusalem. Space was tight and each family had to settle for a one-room mud hut along a dirt alley. Water and resources were in short supply, so one had to learn to share with the neighbors. In such crowded conditions, it was tempting to ignore the weak, the disabled and the elderly who couldn't work, and to expel the sick and diseased lest contamination spread.

Was it this environment that helped Jesus learn that his neighbor was not simply the person next door, but the old woman down the road who needed food and water brought to her? Or was the neighbor a leper in the caves outside the village who needed oil for his sores and longed for friendship? Perhaps Jesus learned about table ministry from his mother, Mary, by watching her invite a blind man for a meal, or sharing what little she had with a widow. Maybe he learned kindness from Joseph while helping him make some children's furniture free of charge for a couple just starting a family. When Jesus was out on his own as a craftsman working in other villages, perhaps he learned to listen to people's grief and sorrows with compassion. Was it during these years that Jesus learned to befriend the poorest of the poor and to make outcasts feel welcome and loved?

Tense Times in Galilee

Tensions were in the air when Jesus was growing up. His people resented the wealthy and corrupt Herod who taxed them heavily so he could build luxurious palaces. There had been several rebellions when Jesus was a boy, but the Romans showed no mercy for troublemakers. Jesus must have heard stories of crucifixions told around campfires at night. As an adult he heard about Pilate, the ruthless Roman procurator who killed some Jews while they were at prayer and had others beaten to death for complaining about taxes. Jesus must have felt anger at the oppression of his people and surely he shared their desire for freedom.

Was it during these early years in Galilee that Jesus learned to defend the poor and the oppressed? Was it then that he resolved to speak out against hypocrisy, greed and injustice? Could it be that in the midst of repression and violence Jesus learned the power of turning the other cheek, the effectiveness of nonviolence against injustice and persecution?

The gospel stories of Jesus' public life are filled with memories of his extraordinary empathy. Mark, who gave us the earliest Gospel, tells a touching story of a man with a "dreaded skin disease" who approached Jesus and knelt before him, saying, "If you want to, you can make me clean." What faith this man had! He did not even know Jesus, and yet he was confident that this young preacher would not be repulsed by his odor or his ravaged condition. He believed that Jesus could heal him and change his whole life back to normal by simply wanting to do it. The story tells us that Jesus was moved with pity toward this utter stranger. Jesus did not back off from him in discomfort or fear. He could feel the pain that this total stranger felt in his affliction. Jesus reached out, touched the man and said simply, "I do choose. Be made clean" (Mark 1:40-45).

Following in His Footsteps

Dorothy Day is a woman of our own time who seemed to have been moved by the Spirit of the Lord to serve the way she did. After her conversion to Catholicism in 1927, she established houses where the poor and homeless were welcome to come, share food at her table and have a safe place to stay. She took in addicts, prostitutes, the elderly and the abandoned. Dorothy herself also had known homelessness and life on the streets, so she could empathize with the pain and anguish of the dispossessed. Like the Master, she reached out to them with a healing touch.

Robert Coles, a child psychologist at Harvard, tells a story about Dorothy Day that demonstrates the solidarity she had with the poor. When he was in graduate school in New York City, his teachers advised him to consult her in his research. He went to the address he had been given and was invited in. As Coles entered, he saw two women talking at a table. One was looking attentively at the other, who was in rags and quite drunk. The woman who was listening excused herself, approached Coles and quietly said, "Are you waiting to talk to one of us?" Coles writes, "One of us: with those three words she cut through layers of self-importance. With those three words she told me what Dorothy Day was all about."

Jesus and Outcasts

Jesus seemed to be especially involved with people who were rejected. As we mentioned earlier, he had learned in Nazareth what it meant to be a marginal person. Jesus was especially concerned about outcasts. In his day, many people were rejected by polite society for one reason or another. Those who were diseased or disabled were often thought to be cursed by God, and so they were avoided as "unclean." Prostitutes, many of whom had been abused as children or divorced by disgruntled husbands, were rejected as sinners who could not be forgiven by God. Tax collectors were generally hated because they worked for the Romans and often bullied and swindled their own Jewish people. Many Jews felt intense alienation toward the occupying Roman soldiers as well as toward other Gentiles. Slaves and the free were often hostile toward each other, as were urban dwellers and peasants. Men felt superior to women, and husbands often viewed their wives as servants and property. As in our own time, each person seemed to have a list of those they deemed inferior and deserving of rejection.

Jesus did not accept these judgments and divisions. For him, each person was a child of God, each a sister and brother. Jesus invited his followers to call him their friend, and he offered his comfort and assistance to all. Whether it was a leper, a hemorrhaging woman, a blind man, a Samaritan woman, a Roman centurion who had lost his daughter or a widow who had buried her only son, Jesus was prepared to do what he could to bring the healing power of God into their lives.

We know that Jesus' generosity was not without cost or risk. Apparently there were those who did not approve of his openness to outcasts. Some resented his amazing capacity to look beyond appearance and sin and see the beauty within each person.

Early in his Gospel, Mark tells a story of Jesus entering the synagogue and meeting a man with a withered hand. Jesus saw that the Pharisees present were just waiting for him to break the Sabbath law by curing this man. That would give them grounds to condemn Jesus. The young preacher could have just said his prayers and minded his own business. Instead, Jesus invited the man to come before the congregation and asked whether it was lawful to save or destroy life on the Sabbath. Mark writes that Jesus was angry and grieved at how heartless these Pharisees were. To teach them that the highest law was love, Jesus asked the man to stretch out his withered hand, and he cured him. Mark says, "The Pharisees went out and immediately conspired with the Herodians against him, how to destroy him" (Mark 3:1-6). Jesus was serious about the importance of loving service: He was even willing to put his life at risk to make his point.

Self-sacrifice

Thomas Merton observed that it is not enough to seek peace and happiness just for ourselves. We also have to be willing to sacrifice so that others can enjoy these gifts of God. Merton came to the conviction that genuine faith had to be concerned about justice. Striking examples of such faith were the four North American women missionaries who were brutally raped and murdered in El Salvador in 1980. One of them, Sister Ita Ford, had written home that she and her fellow missionaries did not hope to bring about any drastic changes. They went to El Salvador simply to walk with the poor and help them in their struggle against injustice.

All of these women followed Jesus' example in giving their lives for others. Sister Dorothy Kazel, one of the martyred women, passed on her spirit to her student, Amy Scott. Amy has been lobbying for the closing of the U.S. Army School of the Americas in Fort Benning, Georgia, where some of the officers who killed these women were trained. Another of the martyrs, Jean Donovan, became a role model for third-graders at St. Michael School in Cincinnati. They signed posters to the families of the four slain women and held a bake sale of Jean's favorite cookies to raise money for the missions. The Spirit of the Lord continues to be among his friends, moving them to serve others.

Service in His Name

Jesus commissioned his followers to spread his gospel of loving and just service to all nations. Service has many faces. It might be a parent staying up all night with a sick child or a teen bringing an elderly grandparent a birthday cake. It might be helping a youngster with homework or loaning a friend some money. For some, carrying out the mission of Jesus means standing up against violence, injustice or degradation of the environment. In all, it is the Spirit of the Lord who is still at work. As Jesus told his disciples after he had washed their feet the night before he died, "Whoever receives one whom I send receives me" (John 13:20a).

For Reflection

- *A saying holds that "there's a big difference between being Church and playing Church." How do you try to "be Church"?*

- *When we enter into an intimate relationship with Jesus, we also take on certain responsibilities that this new friendship demands. What does friendship with Jesus require of you?*

- *On the first Easter evening, Jesus appeared to the disciples in the Upper Room. But his followers didn't recognize him. Then "he showed them his hands and his side" (John 20:20). It was only after seeing his wounds that the disciples recognized their Lord. Some commentators see Jesus' wounds as "proof" or evidence of his ultimate service to others. How do you provide evidence that helps others recognize the presence of Jesus?*

CHAPTER NINE

Jesus, Man of the Earth

Pope John Paul II has repeatedly pointed out that the world is facing an environmental crisis. The oceans and waterways of the world are seriously polluted; toxic chemicals, garbage and even nuclear waste are degrading the land.

In Marmansk, Russia, nuclear submarines are being abandoned in shallow waters and nuclear warheads are being dumped in open fields. What a health horror looms as the radioactive material begins to come in contact with local residents!

Overfishing has endangered the food supply and in places like Newfoundland, where fishing was a way of life. The people are being forced to leave their homeland forever. The protective ozone layer has been torn open, and a hole the size of North America now exposes millions to ultraviolet rays. The burning of fossil fuels fouls our air and creates a "greenhouse effect," which is profoundly affecting global weather patterns.

Reactions to this crisis vary. Some deny its existence and continue to consume and waste. Some feel helpless in the face of such a dilemma and do nothing. Others turn to science with the confidence that it can fix all our problems. But more and more people seem to be turning to the religions of the world, confident that their beliefs and values can help us save the earth from devastation. Many Christians look to Jesus and his teachings to help them rebuild the earth and pass on a healthy environment to their children.

A Man Close to the Earth

Jesus' Jewish faith taught him that all creation came from

the hand of the Creator, all life from the very breath of God. By desert campfires at night, he had heard the stories of how God had been the creator of the heavens, the vast seas, the earth and all living things. At the Temple, he prayed aloud with the thousands of pilgrims: "The heavens are telling the glory of God; and the firmament proclaims his handiwork" (Psalm 19:1). He was aware that "the earth is the Lord's" (Psalm 24:1), and, as a devout Jew, he was aware of his responsibilities to honor that earth as Abba's dwelling place.

Jesus was a rural person, who grew up in Galilee, an area known for its natural beauty, a lush land that had two harvests a year. The hillsides where Jesus walked were filled with sheep grazing on the rich green grasses. Thus his teachings reflect what he had learned about the Creator from nature. His teachings on the loving and saving reign of God are often drawn from images of flowers, birds, fruit, mustard seeds, harvests, the sun, lightning, rain, wind, fish, sheep and other natural phenomena. In his stories and parables, Jesus was not simply using natural images as teaching aids. Rather, he was sharing experiences he had of the loving Creator present in the world. He was encouraging his listeners to discover the movement of their God in the world.

Our God, Abba

Jesus' favorite image of God was Abba, which means "gentle dad." The Hebrew scriptures use the image "Father" a handful of times to describe the Lord God, but they never speak of Abba. The trust and intimacy connoted in the title *Abba* is astounding, unprecedented, and must have come from the intense closeness with God that Jesus experienced in his life with his parents, in quiet hours of prayer and in meeting people of all kinds along the dusty roads of Palestine.

Jesus also seems to have had profoundly moving experiences of his Creator in nature. When he joined his neighbors to plant the spring crops, gather in the harvest, or collect fruit from the trees near Nazareth, Jesus surely would have learned of the love and generosity of the Creator. When

Jesus walked down to Capernaum to bring home fish for the table, he may have recognized in the waters of the Sea of Galilee and the catch of the day just how Abba cares for his children. The gentle breezes off the desert, the quick violent storms over the sea, as well as the beautiful morning sunrises may very well have taught Jesus about life and death, as well as about the love, compassion, beauty and power of Abba. Jesus, devoted to the Hebrew tradition of creation being a good gift from God, would have been a person deeply sensitive to the presence of God in the world about him. Along with his fellow Jews, he prayed that the "heavens are telling the glory of God; and the firmament proclaims his handiwork" (Psalm 19:1).

Lessons From Nature

Many of Jesus' teachings reflect his closeness to nature and the lessons he learned from it. His radical teachings on God's unconditional love of all people, the Creator's forgiving embrace of sinners and the necessity of loving even our enemies are in part drawn from what Jesus learned from creation. Jesus' astounding injunction to love was: "Love your enemies and pray for those who persecute you, so that you may be children of your Father in heaven; for he makes his sun rise on the evil and on the good, and sends rain on the righteous and on the unrighteous" (Matthew 5:44-45).

Jesus compared the free movement of God's Spirit to the mysterious movement of the wind. He paralleled God's generous sharing of the divine word to the sowing of seeds in springtime. In the Sermon on the Mount, Jesus pointed to the wild flowers and birds to demonstrate how Abba's love and care are extended to all creation. The Master proclaimed that Abba's covenant was as it had been promised to Noah, a covenant with everything and everyone that lives on the earth. Jesus proclaimed that Abba's embrace extended from the tiniest sparrow to all the children of the Creator.

Jesus taught that all creation was a gift to be shared and thus encouraged his disciples to share even the shirts off their backs, and to go the second mile and to lend generously

(Matthew 5:4-42). He warned his followers about anxieties over their clothing, drink and food, reminding them that Abba was a generous provider. Jesus said: "Look at the birds of the air... your heavenly Father feeds them...Consider the lilies of the field...even Solomon in all his glory was not clothed like one of these" (Matthew 6:26;28-29).

The Master also knew that, in spite of God's generosity, many people were deprived of adequate food and drink and lacked the resources to live happily. Jesus had watched Herod strip the beautiful forests in order to build magnificent monuments to himself. He had seen the Romans gather the rich resources of Israel and ship them back to Rome. Jesus knew that deprivation did not come from Abba, but from the greed and selfishness of the rich. He therefore warned his followers to give generously to the poor, to avoid hoarding and waste, and to live simply. He strongly warned that riches could be a serious obstacle to entering the kingdom of God. And Jesus taught his disciples that if they first seek the reign of God's love, generosity and compassion, plenty of the earth's bounty would be available for all to share.

Jesus' own experience of greed and the degradation of resources moves him today to compassion for mothers like those in India who bring their children to the rivers for washing and drink, only to find that the waters have been fouled by the factories upstream. The risen Lord is in solidarity with so many indigenous people today who often have to stand by and watch their rich forests burned to the ground and their lands stripped by greedy developers. He can feel for the "little ones" in Australia who suffer health problems from excessive ultraviolet rays coming through the hole in the ozone layer above them. Jesus knows the suffering of the multitudes of people throughout the world who suffer from lack of the basics while others enjoy enormous excess.

Teaching in Parables

Jesus' parables are often drawn from nature and teach his followers about the need to honor the earth. One of Jesus' most powerful parables describes creation as a vineyard (Matthew 1:33-43). The owner of the vineyard had leased the vineyard to others, and at harvest time he sent his servants to receive his share of the grapes. Instead of giving up the grapes, the tenants twice beat up and stone the servants sent on the mission. Finally, the owner sends his own son to obtain justice from the tenants. The tenants brutally murder the son of the owner, and then assume that they are now in possession of the vineyard. Instead, the owner has the greedy tenants killed and leases the vineyard to others who would justly share the harvest.

Jesus' message is clear: Creation is the Lord's, and its resources are to be shared justly. Those who, through injustice, greed and violence, deprive others will ultimately bring death and destruction upon themselves.

In another vineyard parable, Jesus again teaches that this is God's world and that its resources are pure gift (Matthew 20:1-16). In this story, those people who have worked all day in the vineyard complain because they have received the same pay as those who came on the job later in the day. The employer makes it clear that this is his vineyard and his money, and that he has a right to be as generous as he pleases.

Once again Jesus teaches that creation belongs to Abba and that all we receive is gift. All of God's children have a right to their equal share in the earth's resources. The kingdom of God is not to be a place of haves and have-nots, a place where some live in excess while others barely survive. God's gifts are to be shared with equity and justice.

Miracle Stories

Many of the miracle stories teach us about our Creator God. For instance, in Luke's version of the powerful story of the calming of the storm, Jesus and his disciples are crossing the Sea of Galilee when a violent storm suddenly comes upon them. The boat is shipping water, and the disciples begin to panic. They desperately look to Jesus for help, only to find him sound asleep! Jesus awakes to their cries, calmly stands up to calm the storm, and then rebukes his followers for their lack of faith (Luke 8:22-25).

This miracle story has been told for two thousand years. It is a story that teaches that Jesus carries the power of the Creator over nature. In our own time, it teaches us that no matter how much creation is threatened today, the power of Jesus can help his followers heal the earth.

In another nature miracle story, Jesus is described as walking on water (Mark 6:45-52). In Mark's version, Jesus has just fed five thousand people with just five loaves and two fish, and has demonstrated the abundance of God's gifts to people. The disciples had taken one of the boats and sailed for Bethsaida. Jesus stays behind to send the crowd back to their homes, and then he goes to a quiet mountain place to pray. Late that night, the disciples are still out to sea making little headway because of the rough waves. Suddenly they see the Master coming toward them, actually walking on the sea. Jesus tells them not to be afraid, and then gets into the boat as the waters become calm.

Again, Jesus is portrayed as the Lord of nature, a personification of the Creator who has power over nature and who can calm our fears of its destructive forces. Today the story can readily apply to the fears that many of us have over the deterioration of our environment. It is a tale that can help us derive courage from our faith in the power of Jesus.

Mysteries of Jesus' Life

The mysteries of Jesus' life also have much to teach us in this time when the very life of the earth is threatened. The birth of Jesus reveals that God was incarnated, made flesh and became one with the material, physical world. John's Gospel proclaims: "God so loved the world that he gave his only Son" (John 3:16a). What more do we need in order to recognize the sanctity of human life—indeed of all life?

Jesus' death has conquered darkness, sin and evil. Jesus' brutal execution became one of the events that saved the world. He had proclaimed that he was the "life of the world," and was willing to offer his life that all might have life (John 6:51).

And finally, in raising Jesus from the dead, God transformed the physical body of Jesus and at the same time manifested the ultimate fulfillment destined for humans as well as for creation. God did not create in order to ultimately destroy in fire, but to bring all to fulfillment. The Spirit of the Risen Lord gives us a glimpse of the endtime, when the just and all the earth will be brought to completion in eternal life.

For Reflection

- *Concerns about ecology and the environment have moved many religious orders in recent years to become directly involved in eco-justice initiatives—from establishing and running organic farms to sponsoring recycling centers. Should such efforts be a priority for Christians? Why or why not?*

- *It is a Christian belief that as a result of the incarnation all creation is suffused with the presence of God. Name some ways that Christians recognize and honor this divine presence.*

- *A long-standing belief, especially in the Eastern Churches, is that all creation is undergoing a process of divinization—a reversal of the destructive power of humanity's original sin. If this is true, how do you reconcile this belief with what appears to be evidence that, ecologically, creation is deteriorating?*

CHAPTER TEN

Jesus and Freedom

The poor *campesinos* in the mountains of El Salvador have a great deal to teach us about Jesus. Several years ago, my son, B.J., and I visited there, and the faces and hearts of these people spoke to us about the Master. Their small clay-brick houses and simple clothes spoke of a life-style similar to that which Jesus must have experienced. The simple food they so generously shared reminded us of the Lord's table ministry. Their weathered faces and calloused hands revealed the hard work that Jesus the carpenter must have known.

You could see the deep lines of grief and loss in the faces of the parents whose children had "disappeared" into torture and death. One could see that these people knew of crucifixion. Their processions to bury their dead while singing *"Presente"* ("they are still present with us") showed us their strong belief in resurrection. As we witnessed their deep faith and listened to accounts of their struggle against oppression and violence, we learned of a strong and courageous Jesus who was the source of their courage and hope.

The Importance of Freedom

I once had the privilege of spending some time with Father Bernard Häring, one of the great moral theologians of this century. He was then writing his three-volume work on morality, which was to be called *Free and Faithful in Christ*. When I asked him why he chose that title, he said, "Freedom is at the heart of the gospel." I knew that this was a lesson learned from experience.

At an earlier age, Father Häring had been forced to serve as a medic in the armed forces of Nazi Germany, risked his life secretly serving as a priest and spent time in a Russian prison camp. I heard his words as words of wisdom, for they came from a saintly and learned priest who spent his life writing about and living the gospel.

It has been said that one of the reasons why Christianity spread so rapidly was that it offered what so many of the poor and oppressed people were looking for—freedom. Did that mean that conversion resulted in slaves being released by their owners or that the poor became wealthy or powerful? Not really. Did it mean that people who had been oppressed were treated any better because of their Baptism? Probably not. In fact, following Jesus often brought on additional persecution. Did conversion restore the disabled or those suffering from disease or illness to wholeness and health? Not usually.

Then what did Jesus mean when he told his followers: "If you continue in my word, you are truly my disciples, and you will know the truth, and the truth will make you free...you will be free indeed" (John 8:32,36)? What did Paul the apostle mean when he wrote to the Galatians, "you were called to freedom" (Galatians 5:13)? What is this Christian freedom which Jesus offers to those who follow him? In this chapter we will look at Christian freedom as Jesus' call to be free from attachments and self-centeredness, his call to be faithful to God.

Freedom From Attachments

Jesus' own life was one of simplicity. Luke's nativity story tells us that Jesus was born in a manger, a sign of his plain and humble beginnings. Jesus grew up in simple surroundings and spent most of his years working with his hands. Jesus had some hard sayings regarding attachment to things. He once warned a scribe who wanted to follow him that he could promise little comfort or security. Jesus said, "Foxes have holes and birds of the air have nests; but the Son of Man has nowhere to lay his head" (Matthew 8:20).

The Sermon on the Mount contains some of Jesus' strongest teachings about living simply. On our recent pilgrimage to

Jesus' own homeland, we had the privilege of sitting on that magnificent hillside where Jesus preached overlooking the Sea of Galilee. The Master's presence can still be felt on that hillside, and as we read Matthew's version of the sermon, it was as though Jesus' words still echoed through the trees.

Jesus began with the startling words: "Blessed are the poor in spirit" (Matthew 5:3). The "poor in spirit" in the Hebrew Scriptures are those who are without material possessions and who place their trust and hope in God. These are the "little ones," the outcasts for whom Jesus seemed to have such a special affection. They were blessed or "holy" because Abba is with them, loving them tenderly and giving them strength to endure.

Jesus instructed his followers not to store up treasures on earth, but rather to store up treasures in heaven. Then he wisely observed, "For where your treasure is, there your heart will be also...You cannot serve God and wealth" (Matthew 6:21,24).

Jesus told his followers not to have anxiety about anything, whether it be food, clothing, or even life itself. He counseled his disciples to share their goods with the poor and to travel light. He warned them that riches could be an obstacle to salvation. Jesus told his disciples to place their lives in the hands of Abba and take one day at a time. Jesus' call to freedom offers liberation from the anxieties and stresses that so many of us feel today. It is an invitation to peace of mind, inner joy and the trust that comes from detachment from things and from knowing that God is with us no matter what happens.

Recently I visited members of a small faith community in our parish. We talked about our life in the suburbs. Here we were, a group of people who had nice homes, good jobs, financial security. And yet most of us, like Martha in the gospels, were "worried and distracted by many things" (Luke 10:41). Many of us felt caught in a consumer way of life, surrounded by malls and megastores and constantly accumulating things that we really did not need. Most of our households had two incomes, and we found that we spent most of our concern and energy working both in and outside the home, keeping up with the bills, taking care of the children and myriad other activities.

We felt rather overwhelmed by it all and wanted more time with our spouses and children—time to think, to pray and to reach out to others. We realized that we needed to be more detached, live more simply and share more of what we have with the poor. That night we decided that we would take stock of our priorities and our life-styles. We all prayed that we would begin to take Jesus' example and teaching more seriously. We asked for the freedom that Jesus promised his followers.

Freedom From Self-centeredness

Jesus was a person devoted to others. In his short public life he was daily preoccupied with curing the sick, healing the disabled, cleansing lepers, bringing forgiveness to sinners and driving evil spirits out of people. We find him defending outcasts against those who oppress them and decrying the fact that many of his people were being misled by hypocritical religious leaders. Jesus intensely trained his close disciples and often spent his days instructing and feeding huge gatherings of people. We find him sometimes conversing at night with a scribe or Pharisee who had sought him out. We read about his visits to the houses of friends and dinners with Pharisees and tax collectors.

Even when Jesus was being arrested in the garden, he was concerned about the release of his disciples. On the way to Calvary, Jesus told the women who cried for him to turn their sorrow to their own children. Suffering on the cross, he took time to promise salvation to the thief next to him. And before he died to save the world from sin, Jesus gave over his own mother to the Beloved Disciple. There is no life in human history that has ever been so giving and self-sacrificing.

Think of the countless disciples who have tried to imitate Jesus' selflessness. Many followers of Jesus today have left the security of their homes to serve the poor in areas that are often squalid and dangerous.

I recently read of Yvonne Dilling, a young woman who risked her life to help Salvadoran children cross a flooded river into the safety of neighboring Honduras in 1985. She made dozens of trips carrying children on her back through raging waters. Several times she nearly drowned with the children clinging to her, and on one trip she and the children were fired on from a helicopter.

Or one thinks of the many heroic people who respond to emergency calls, or of our firefighters or police who often have to risk their lives to save others.

Many unsung heroes run shelters for the homeless or work tirelessly in soup kitchens. Jesus' spirit of self-sacrifice is still alive in many of his followers today.

Free to Be Faithful

Jesus was single-minded about being faithful to the will of his God. During his temptations in the desert, he made it clear to the devil that he would only worship and serve the Lord God. In the synagogue in Nazareth, Jesus proclaimed that he had been anointed by the Spirit of the Lord to preach to the poor and bring freedom to those held captive or oppressed. He allowed no one, not even his closest apostles, to deter him or to lead him to violence or the ambition for power. Jesus was determined to carry out his mission of teaching that love, forgiveness, and sacrifice offered the way to eternal life. And he asked the same of his followers. He said, "If any want to become my followers, let them deny themselves and take up their cross daily and follow me. For those who want to save their life will lose it, and those who lose their life for my sake will save it" (Luke 9:23-24).

Jesus was faithful to the end. He freed himself from the normal human doubts and anxieties of life. Jesus was able to get beyond the frustration he must have felt when even his own apostles did not seem to understand his message. He was able to rise above the fears that caused him to sweat blood in the garden. Jesus was able to pray his way through the abandonment he felt on the cross. At the finish of his life he said, "Father, into your hands I commend my spirit" (Luke 23:46).

Modern Freedom Crusader

In 1947, the year before the infamous apartheid policy was enforced in South Africa, a young Catholic bishop named Denis Hurley was ordained. The motto on his coat of arms was, "Where the Spirit is, there is freedom." For the next half century, this young prelate courageously stood against apartheid and opposed the unjust oppression of the blacks in his country. Naturally Archbishop Hurley drew much opposition. His home was firebombed, the government threatened at one point to ban him and his enemies branded him with every label from "Communist" to an "ecclesiastical Che Guevara." But like his model, Jesus, Archbishop Hurley never faltered but sustained the freedom and courage to continue his efforts against injustice. Ironically, the system of apartheid that he had fought throughout his years in office came to an end in 1994, the same year that he retired as archbishop. He had served his people well. Now in his eighties, Archbishop Hurley continues to minister to the poor in an inner-city parish in Durban.

Jesus calls us to freedom: from slavish attachments, from the prison of selfishness, from our sins and our fears. He promises to give us the freedom of the children of God so that we can reach out to those in need.

For Reflection

- *Jesus teaches us in the Gospels that we must be free of things in order to be free to love and serve others. In other words, people and relationships are (or ought to be) a priority for Christians. How do you disengage yourself from things in order to concentrate on being Jesus for others?*

- *List five things you can do to "live more simply so that others may simply live."*

- *Jesus never hands us our crosses. According to the gospel, we must pick up our own crosses. When have you picked up your cross?*

CHAPTER ELEVEN

Jesus, Liberator

The image of Jesus as liberator is not a new one. Jesus himself promised his disciples that the truth that he taught them would set them free. He assured them that "if the Son makes you free, then you will be free indeed" (John 8:36). It would certainly seem that the very heart of Jesus' mission in life was to liberate people from their sins, their disabilities, and from any attachments that would keep them from being one with God. This same image of the Lord moved Paul to proclaim to the early Christians: "Where the Spirit of the Lord is, there is freedom" and "Christ has set us free" (2 Corinthians 3:17; Galatians 5:1).

The oppressed in Central and Latin America have reclaimed the image of Jesus as liberator and have reinvigorated its depth and power. When I visited El Salvador with my son at the end of the recent war, I could see how Jesus had freed his followers there in so many ways. I could see it in the lined faces of the *Madres*, the mothers of the disappeared. These women met everyday in a downtown office that had been bombed and terrorized, and they worked to identify victims of the government and bring the killers to justice. These women had been freed from bitterness and from fear, even from fear of death. These women had a dedication and courage like I had never experienced before. I also listened to the *campesinos* who lived in the mountains tell me how Jesus had freed them from despair when they had to live for months underground during the bombings and artillery attacks. I visited the garden where the six Jesuits and two women had been tortured and killed and was told how they defended the poor even though they knew it might cost them their lives.

The icon of such liberation in our time is Archbishop Oscar Romero, who stood in solidarity with his people in their struggle for freedom. By nature a timid and scholarly man, Archbishop Romero had a love of Jesus that freed him from his conservative nature and lack of aggressiveness. When his priest-friend Rutilio Grande was gunned down along with an old man and boy, Romero suddenly stopped criticizing the resistance movement and was transformed into a prophetic firebrand who confronted the highest authorities in his country. He knew that his position would eventually seal his fate. Death threats alerted him that he would pay dearly for his actions. And yet Romero lost all fear, even the fear for his life. He once proclaimed that though his enemies would kill him, he would rise again in his people.

One of the most powerful stories I heard of Jesus the liberator in El Salvador concerned a lovely young woman named Maria. During the war she had taken up the cause of her people and spent her days taking care of orphans, feeding the poor and signing up people to vote for an honest government. The government saw Maria as a threat and sent a death squad to terrorize her. The soldiers beat her, raped her and then took her out to the garbage dump. They shouted obscenities at her and told her to kneel down and promise never to oppose the government again. Maria refused to submit, was shot to death, falling dead in the refuse. The poor of the village came, gathered up her body, washed it and carried it to church. As they processed the villagers sang her name and each time proclaimed *"Presenté"* ("she is still with us"). Maria never gave up her freedom, and she was now liberated even from death to enjoy eternal life with her Lord.

The Historical Jesus

Liberation theology gives a renewed attention to the historical Jesus and points up his own personal freedom as well as his dedication to the freeing of others. especially outcasts. In the Gospels, the Nazarene is described as a young man who lived much like today's *campesinos*. Like them, Jesus grew up in a one-room mud house in a small village. He had to work most of his life with his hands as a craftsman. Around the age of thirty, Jesus felt the need to separate himself from anything that would distract him from his calling. He left his home, his beloved mother and the very trade from which he had made a living in order to preach a new gospel. He once pointed out that he did not even have a place that he could call his own, where he could lay his head. He and his followers lived frugally off the donations of others as they traveled from place to place teaching and preaching.

When Jesus was arrested, all that he owned was the tunic on his back, and even that was divided among his executioners. When he died, Jesus had to be buried in a grave donated by one of his followers, Joseph of Arimathea. Jesus had lived and died as a person whose only attachment was to his people, whom he loved beyond measure. And once Jesus was raised from the dead, he appeared to his disciples, now free from space and time, hunger and temptation, suffering, and even death itself. He was now free to enjoy the risen life and to share this gift with all those who followed him.

Jesus Freed the Poor

The people of the world who are attracted to Jesus as liberator point out that not only was he poor and oppressed himself, but he also was known as a champion of the downtrodden and marginal. As one *campesino* said to me in Mexico: "Jesus knows what we are going through because he experienced poverty and oppression in his own life."

Jesus experienced firsthand the plight of the common folk in his own tiny village of Nazareth and in the towns and villages that he visited. As mentioned earlier, he saw how the Romans had driven his people from the rich land along the Mediterranean and forced them to eke out a living as tenant farmers. He experienced firsthand the exorbitant taxes and land mortgages that Herod extorted from the Jews of Galilee. Jesus had seen his neighbors imprisoned, sold into slavery, even crucified for not being able to pay what was demanded of them.

And he saw the roads lined with the crucified who had in any way spoken up or rebelled against their persecutors. No doubt Jesus was moved to pity by how lepers and the disabled were cast aside and abandoned. He also witnessed how many women were treated as property. He knew women who had been abused by their fathers or thrown out of their homes by their husbands and often then forced into prostitution as the only means of surviving.

Jesus told the poor and the outcast that they were "blessed." By this he did not mean that their hunger and squalor were gifts from God to be cherished. Rather, Jesus was telling the oppressed that their loving Abba was with them in their suffering, was feeling along with them every inch of the way. Jesus told those who were poor economically or spiritually that they could count on their Abba God to give them the courage and the strength to rise above their suffering with hope. Jesus also let all people know that the Son of Man loved them, lived for them and would die for them.

Jesus freed those who were afflicted from their disabilities. He tossed aside the views that God punished or tested with physical infirmities and witnessed to a God who wanted people to be whole, to be healed. The Gospels overflow with stories of the blind, the crippled, the diseased of mind and body who came to Jesus and were healed of their afflictions. The Gospel of Matthew proclaims: "Then Jesus went about all the cities and villages, teaching in their synagogues, and proclaiming the good news of the kingdom, and curing every disease and every sickness. When he saw the crowds, he had compassion for them, because they were harassed and helpless, like sheep without a shepherd" (Matthew 9:35-37).

Jesus Freed Sinners

Jesus also offered liberation for those imprisoned in sinful habits, those whose spirits were impoverished. Those who today follow liberation theology would say that he attempted to free both the oppressed and oppressors. Jesus prophetically pointed out the judgment that greed, lust, selfishness, self-righteousness and violence brings upon one's spirit.

He told the selfish rich that they had about as much chance of gaining the kingdom of God as a camel would have getting through the eye of a needle. Jesus warned the rich that they could not serve both God and wealth, and he advised them to "store up for yourselves treasures in heaven, where neither moth nor rust consumes and where thieves do not break in and steal. For where your treasure is, there your heart will be also" (Matthew 6:20-21). In one of his strongest statements, Jesus warned against clinging to anything other than their savior: "For what will it profit them if they gain the whole world but forfeit their life?" (Matthew 16:26).

Jesus warned corrupt and sinful religious leaders that they must be humble servants of their people. The Master did not mince words as he described some of the scribes and Pharisees as hypocrites who did not practice what they preached. Jesus chastises these leaders, who lay heavy burdens upon others and proudly strut in public, demanding the first places at banquets and in the synagogues. He called such leaders blind guides, blind fools and hypocrites, snakes and white-washed tombs filled with death and filth (Matthew 23:1-37). Jesus called these leaders to repentance as he cried over the city of Jerusalem, wishing that he could gather his people to himself as innocent children.

Jesus taught his own followers the authentic way to exercise power and leadership. He warned them not to be tyrants, but to be humble leaders dedicated to service. This was the very example he gave in his own leadership and Jesus expected no less from them. His teaching was: "[W]hoever wishes to be great among you must be your servant, and whoever wishes to be the first among you must be your slave, just as the Son of Man came not to be served but to serve, and to give his life a ransom for many" (Matthew 20:2-28).

Jesus and Political Freedom

Many disciples of Jesus in developing countries are victims of political oppression and look to his teaching and his power

79

to guide them in their resistance to corrupt governments. Those who thus see Jesus' teaching as relevant to political issues are often charged with mixing religion and politics, the Church with the State. Liberation theologians are often accused of projecting their own political agenda on to Jesus, whose sole concern was supposedly religious reform.

The question here is: "Was Jesus political?"

Well, first of all it is apparent that Jesus was not politically militant in the modern sense. The Gospels give no indication that Jesus resisted the Roman occupation of his land or put together any revolutionary plans for his followers to carry out. Even though he was probably crucified for political crimes, there is no evidence that such charges against him were true. It would, therefore, be anachronistic and a distortion of Jesus' teachings of love, compassion and forgiveness to portray him as being a modern freedom fighter.

At the same time, it must be pointed out that, in Jesus' time, there was no clear distinction between religion and politics. In fact, the two were integrally related. Rome's domination over Israel had many religious implications, and the Romans often attempted to enforce their symbols and laws on the Jews. Conversely, the Jews saw Roman domination as having many religious implications and longed for a kind of freedom that would be both political and religious. Thus when Jesus criticized the Jewish religious leadership, he knew full well that they were Roman-appointed puppets and that his verbal attacks would have both religious and political repercussions. When it did come time for his conviction, we see both the Sanhedrin and the Roman court cooperating.

Those who view Jesus as a liberator maintain that his gospel teaching has relevance to both religious and political reform. They view Jesus as one committed to justice on all levels of life and readily see Jesus and his teachings as confrontational toward political oppression, terrorism and corruption. This, of course, was the genius of Archbishop Romero, who was able to discern how the life and teachings of Jesus stood in opposition to the cruelty, violence and oppression that the government was inflicting on the Salvadoran people. It is the view also of former Anglican Archbishop Desmond Tutu of South Africa, who confronted the evil system of apartheid with the teachings of Jesus and who more recently brought the gospel teaching on forgiveness and reconciliation to both oppressed and oppressors in his country.

Freeing Us

The image of Jesus as liberator has spread through the globe today to Africa, Asia, Eastern Europe and other areas of the globe. In this country, Jesus is called upon to free the impoverished in Appalachia, the homeless in our inner cities and the disabled who have been marginalized. Jesus has kept his word and is indeed offering us the power and grace to free ourselves and others *from* injustice, sin, poverty and violence. He is the savior who frees us *for* a future of global peace, hope and justice which is needed throughout the globe.

For Reflection

- *Pope John Paul II and other Church leaders have been highly critical of liberation theology and those who profess it because it often draws on Marxist doctrine. What dangers, if any, do you see in liberation theology? What are the positive aspects of this theology, if any?*

- *The poor and the oppressed often see themselves in the gospel accounts of Jesus. As the Mexican campesino mentioned in this chapter said, "Jesus knows what we are going through." How can this perception serve both the poor and the rich in dealing with the issues of poverty and oppression?*

- *It is often said that Jesus came to save persons (bodies, souls and spirits) not just souls. Do you agree or disagree with this concept? Why or why not?*

CHAPTER TWELVE

The Baptism of Jesus

R ecently my family and I witnessed a blessed event. It was
not the birth of a baby, but the rebirth in Baptism of our
newest nephew, Liam. Soon after he was born, Liam was
christened at an inspiring celebration. I think it was the
expression on the face of this infant after his Baptism that I shall
always remember the most vividly. His tiny face was lit up with
such joy and excitement that one would think that he really felt
the grace and love of the Lord in his little heart.

Our prayers for Liam were many that morning. We thanked
the Spirit of the Lord for this newly beloved son of God and
asked God to protect him and strengthen him against the many
temptations he will face. We welcomed this little one into our
Church community and hoped that he would carry on Jesus'
mission.

An Ancient Ritual

In bathing Liam in the waters of Christian Baptism that
morning, we were recalling the baptism of Jesus in the river
Jordan two millennia ago. On that occasion, a young ascetic
whom people called John the Baptist was causing quite a stir.
This prophet must have cut a striking figure as he emerged
from the desert dressed in ragged camel hair, his body lean
from a diet of only wild honey and locusts. Like the prophets of
old, this young hermit called his people to repentance for their
sins.

Many scholars think that John the Baptist mentored Jesus,
teaching him the ways of the desert and alerting him to signs of
the "reign of God" (Luke 3:6). John may have inspired the

83

young carpenter, Jesus, to stand up to hypocrisy and to be willing to die rather than give up his principles. As we know, both men were executed by rulers who hated them for exposing hypocrisy and unjust oppression. John was beheaded, and Jesus was crucified.

The Baptist seems to have grown in awe of his young protegé, Jesus. John told the people at the Jordan that his mission was now to prepare the way for one greater and worthier than he. And when John saw Jesus coming to be baptized, he seemed embarrassed and remarked that it would be more fitting if Jesus were baptizing him. Jesus insisted, however, and entered the waters of repentance.

Now it was not as though Jesus needed to repent for an evil past or have his sins washed away. But Jesus apparently did want to show his friendship with sinners, his solidarity with those who suffered from evil and his commitment to compassion and forgiveness. The scene after Jesus' baptism is recounted in all four Gospels, obviously drawn from a memory long treasured among his disciples. Mark's Gospel, which is the earliest written, tells of Jesus' coming out of the river, seeing the heavens open and feeling the Spirit of God descending upon him. Jesus then heard a voice from the heavens saying, "You are my Son, the Beloved; with you I am well pleased" (Mark 1:10-11).

This open-armed and accepting love was given to Jesus by the very source of love itself, his Father. This deep awareness that he was pleasing to and loved by God the Father gave Jesus the courage to face the demons of temptation in the desert and the challenges of a new life as preacher and healer. The presence of this loving Spirit in his life enabled him to teach the truth and bring the healing and forgiving power of God to others. Knowing that he was loved sustained Jesus when he was abandoned by his own followers. It gave him the courage even to endure the horrors of crucifixion. No matter what happened to Jesus, he could go on because he knew he would always be loved by his Father.

Mark's Gospel does not allow for any fanfare after Jesus' baptism. The young Galilean carpenter was immediately led by the Spirit into the desert to face and overcome evil temptations. Then, upon hearing that his mentor, John the Baptist, had been arrested, Jesus took up his own mission of preaching repentance, chose his first disciples and began to perform the first of many healings.

The Gospel in Miniature

This magnificent story of Jesus' baptism sums up the Christian life: It is the gospel in miniature. The story speaks of our sinfulness, of our need for repentance and forgiveness. At the same time, the story reveals that our God loves us and is pleased with us as sons and daughters. It shows us that we can face any desert of depression, abandonment or loss because we are loved by a God who will never let us down. The story calls each of us to step up, to carry on the mission of bringing the good news of love and forgiveness to our families, our neighbors—indeed, to anyone sent our way by the Spirit.

At the heart of it all seems to be that one line that Jesus heard from his Abba, "You are my Son, the Beloved; with you I am well pleased" (Luke 3:22).

I recently had dinner with an older gentleman who helped me understand why this experience of being loved is so important. "Uncle Bud," as so many of his friends call him, is a person who has spent most of his life and much of his money helping people who have hit bottom from alcoholism, drug addiction, depression, or even crime. Often he has invited these people into his own home and cared for them until they were well on their way to being healed. Many of them he put through school and helped to get jobs. Uncle Bud told me that he had reached out to all kinds of people from troubled teens to hardened criminals. He said that he always wondered what all these people had in common. What were they all looking for that would give them peace and happiness?

That night over dinner, the elderly gentleman looked across the table at me, his eyes sparkling with goodness, and said, "After many years, I finally concluded that all of them wanted to be loved simply for who they were."

Experiencing the love of the Spirit of God is at the heart of Baptism. Baptismal promises commit the followers of Jesus to offer others this same experience of unconditional love and acceptance. Spouses yearn to know that they are loved and are pleasing to their mates. Children need to know daily that they are beloved daughters and sons, that their parents are pleased with them and will always be there for them. Employees, students, patients, customers: All people come alive when they realize they are loved. Jesus' command at his Last Supper was, "Love one another. Just as I have loved you, you also should love one another" (John 13:34).

Water: Central Symbol

From the very beginning of the Church, Baptism has been the rite of initiation for those wanting to be disciples of Jesus. At Pentecost, Peter spoke out, "Jesus of Nazareth, a man attested to you by God with deeds of power, wonders, and signs that God did through him among you...." Peter reminded his listeners that Jesus was crucified and was raised up by God. He then called the people to repent and come to the waters of Baptism (Acts 2:22-24;38).

Water is the central symbol in the ritual of Baptism. Water is a basic resource, necessary for drinking, washing, growing food; indeed, for sustaining all life.

The symbol of water is important in Scripture. Genesis describes how creation came about when the Spirit swept over the primordial oceans. The Lord saved Noah from the great flood; led the Israelites out of Egypt, dividing the waters of the sea for them; and guided his people safely across the Jordan into the Promised Land.

In the Book of Ezekiel the Lord says, "I will sprinkle clean water upon you, and you shall be clean from all your uncleanesses, and from all your idols I will cleanse you. A new heart I will give you and a new spirit I will put within you.... Then you shall live in the land that I gave your ancestors; and you shall be my people, and I will be your God" (Ezekiel 36:25-26;28).

Water stories abound in the New Testament: Jesus washes the sick in a healing pool, calms a storm, saves Peter from drowning and helps his disciples with miraculous catches of fish. Jesus taught his night visitor, Nicodemus the Pharisee, that he must be born again of water and the Spirit. The Master promised living water to the Samaritan woman, and proclaimed to his disciples, "Let anyone who is thirsty come to me" (John 7:37b). When Jesus' body was pierced after his death, water symbolically flowed from his side. And after Jesus was raised from the dead, he cooked breakfast for his disciples after they had come ashore from a night of fishing. Each of these stories speaks of water in terms of the healing and saving power of the Lord and can be linked with faith and the waters of Baptism.

In the Gospels, Jesus adds other nuances to the meaning of baptism. When his two young apostles, James and John, rather naively and ambitiously asked Jesus if they could sit on the left and right of his throne in the kingdom, Jesus answered with irony, "You do not know what you are asking. Are you able to drink the cup that I drink, or be baptized with the baptism that I am baptized with?" (Mark 10:38). On another occasion, Jesus said, "I have a baptism with which to be baptized, and what stress I am under until it is completed" (Luke 12:50). In both cases, Jesus seemed to refer to the suffering and death he was to endure. He teaches that Baptism calls one to sacrifice and possibly even to persecution.

Oil is another symbol in the baptismal ritual. In the East, oil has been important as a food as well as a cleansing and healing agent. Kings and priests were anointed with oil and the Messiah was expected to come as the anointed one of God, the Christ. So the anointing at Baptism with the sacred oil carries many rich meanings of being cleansed, healed, nurtured and joined to the Christ.

Baptism Today

It is still our custom as Catholics to have our babies baptized soon after birth. No longer is this because we believe they will go to limbo if they die unbaptized. (The authors of the

Catechism of the Catholic Church do not mention limbo and express trust in the mercy of God to save unbaptized infants.) Our infants are brought to the waters of Baptism because we want them to be uniquely graced with the friendship of the Lord. We want them to belong to the community of Jesus' followers from the very beginning of their lives.

As for the many adults whom we welcome into the Catholic Church each year through parish catechumenates, we want them also to know what it means to be pleasing to and loved by God and his disciples. They are invited to repent and to be washed of past sins. They are welcomed into Christian communities who praise and serve the Lord in today's world.

Baptism gifts the Liams and Uncle Buds of the world with the Spirit of the Lord. It enabled people like Dorothy Day and Mother Teresa of Calcutta to see Christ in the poor and the homeless. Baptism empowers the many hidden disciples who serve Jesus each day. It is a sign of repentance, forgiveness, acceptance and love. Baptism is the celebration of a new creation in our hearts of the joy and peace that come from the Spirit. The loving affirmation we received from God at our Baptism continues to give us strength to face life with courage and loving hearts.

For Reflection

- *God's love for us is unconditional; it comes to us without any strings attached. When have you experienced God's unconditional love? Another person's unconditional love? Who do you love unconditionally? Why?*

- *In ancient Antioch, followers of Jesus were first called "Christians"—followers of the Christ, the Anointed One. In a very real way, we Christians are "anointed ones" because we are anointed at Baptism with oil and the Holy Spirit. What does being "anointed" mean to you? What should it mean to people who are not Christians?*

- *After his baptism, Jesus was immediately tempted by the devil to turn away from his mission by committing sins of pride and power.*

But Jesus did not succumb to the temptation because he knew that he was God's Beloved One. When did God's love sustain you during a time of trial or temptation?

CHAPTER THIRTEEN

Jesus and the Eucharist

It was a simple and at the same time an unfathomable gesture. A young preacher, Jesus of Nazareth, took bread and wine and shared it with his friends, saying that this food was indeed himself. He then asked them to continue to share this meal in his memory after he was gone. As a result, after Jesus' resurrection, small groups of early Christians, often at the risk of their lives, began to meet in homes for the "breaking of the bread."

Eventually throngs of Christians gathered for magnificent liturgies in basilicas and cathedrals. To this day, the Eucharist remains the centerpiece of Catholic life: the celebration where disciples give thanks for the risen Lord's presence in their midst, "commune" with Christ and each other, and receive the spiritual nourishment they need to be faithful and serving disciples.

Table Ministry

As a Jew, Jesus was familiar with the fellowship meals of his people. Families and small communities gathered on occasion to pray, share bread and wine, and strengthen their covenant with God and each other. Jesus would have been accustomed to sharing such meals with Mary and Joseph in Nazareth. No doubt he learned early from these meals about the love that God had for people. As he shared bread with his mother, he must have felt nourished by her faith and love. When Joseph passed the cup to Jesus, the boy surely felt his parent's strong protection and care. From them Jesus learned that food and drink could be powerful symbols of self-giving, sacrifice and thanksgiving.

When Jesus started public life, he made sure that such meals would be integral to his ministry. The Gospels reflect many memories of Jesus' "table ministry" where he profoundly changed people's lives and nourished their spirits with his presence.

Luke's Gospel tells of Jesus stopping for a meal in Bethany at the home of close friends Martha, Mary and Lazarus. This meal has special significance, for it symbolizes how Jesus believed that women were as worthy as men to hear his teaching, and that he uniquely chose women to be his disciples. At the meal, Jesus taught Martha that the "one thing" important in life was to enjoy his presence and listen to his word (Luke 10:38-42). We hear more of these friends of Jesus later when he returned to their home in Bethany to raise Lazarus from the dead, talked with Martha about his own resurrection and Mary brought many to believe in him (John 11:45). At another meal in Bethany, it was Mary who anointed Jesus' feet with precious oil and dried them with her hair. When Judas fussed that this was a waste of precious oil, Jesus remarked that Mary had, in fact, anointed his body for burial (John 12:1-8). Profound things happened to people when they dined with Jesus.

A pilgrimage that I took to Jericho helped me understand the meaning of the meal that Jesus had in that town with the diminutive and corrupt tax collector, Zacchaeus. I stood with my fellow pilgrims on a hillside overlooking sycamore trees similar to the one Zacchaeus climbed so that he would see Jesus when he came to town one day. My wife, Marie, who has a talent for role-playing, stood before us on that brilliantly sunny day and, for a few minutes, was Zacchaeus.

Through Marie's twentieth-century voice, Zacchaeus told us of the excitement he felt when he learned of Jesus' impending arrival. He shared his surprise when Jesus beckoned him to come down from his perch in a tree. He told us of his astonishment (as well as that of all the people whom he had extorted over the years) when Jesus honored him by being a guest in his house. Zacchaeus recalled how his heart was moved as he sat at table with Jesus; never before had he felt such love and mercy. He told how Jesus had brought salvation to his house. Zacchaeus said how amazed he was when he heard himself pledge to give half of all he owned to the poor, and return fourfold to those whom he had defrauded. A meal with Jesus can radically change one's life!

One other Gospel story of Jesus' table ministry is especially touching. Here the meal is a "men only" affair at the house of Simon the Pharisee. Given Jesus' stormy relationships with Pharisees, it is rather surprising that he was invited to recline with them at table. During the course of the dinner a "sinful woman" stood behind Jesus and wept. She washed his feet with her tears, dried them with her flowing hair and then proceeded to kiss Jesus' feet and anoint them with precious oil. Someone else might have been embarrassed, but Jesus remained quite calm and even dismissed the mumbling of the other men. He chided them for their lack of hospitality and proceeded to lift up this woman as an example of how deeply love and forgiveness can affect one's life. It is unlikely that either the Pharisees or the woman ever forgot that night's meal with the young carpenter from Nazareth.

The Last Supper

The climactic meal of Jesus' ministry was the Last Supper with his disciples the night before his horrible execution on a cross. The Synoptic Gospels place this meal at Passover. Rumors were circulating that Jesus was to be betrayed, and plots were being made to do away with this young preacher and healer. There was confusion, fear and anxiety among those gathered with Jesus that night at table. Jesus himself seemed sad and pensive. Particularly woeful toward the disciple who was about to betray him, Jesus cried out: "It would have been better for that one not to have been born" (Mark 14:21).

In the midst of this meal, which at the same time remembered the Hebrew Exodus and tensely anticipated the horrors of crucifixion, Jesus did something quite unheard of. He identified the bread and wine that he gave to his disciples with himself, his upcoming death and the kingdom that was to come. Luke's Gospel tells us that Jesus also told his followers to continue celebrating this meal in his memory.

Even after Jesus' death and resurrection, he continued his table ministry. On one occasion the risen Lord joined two of his disciples on the road to Emmaus and revealed his identity to them in the breaking of the bread. On another, he joined his followers for a meal in Jerusalem and instructed them in his messiahship. John's Gospel tells a charming story in which the disciples have returned to their former trade of fishing after Jesus' death. Jesus helps them with a miraculous catch and then actually cooks breakfast for them on the shore. It is after this meal that Jesus touchingly asks Peter three times if he loves him (John 21:4-19).

Ever since those early days two thousand years ago, Christians have treasured the Eucharist, a sacrament with many facets. Eucharist is a sacred meal with the risen Lord and his community. It is an occasion to intimately experience the Master's presence. Eucharist is a celebration of redemption through Jesus' sacrifice on Calvary. It is a time to offer thanksgiving and praise to the Creator God. The eucharistic liturgy is an occasion to be in communion with the Lord, with the local community, and with people all over the world, especially those who suffer.

Sister Jose Hobday, a woman who has shared her Native American and Franciscan heritage with so many, tells of how a meal changed her way of looking at things. When she was small, her mother invited a woman with cancer to Thanksgiving dinner. Jose remembers that she wanted to skip the meal because the woman had such a sickening smell about her, but her mother insisted that Jose be there. Jose recalls that as the sick woman passed the sweet potatoes, she noticed that there would not be enough for Jose and thus did not take any for herself. Young Jose was struck by the kindness of the woman and offered her half of her potato. She also became aware that after this sharing she never noticed the woman's smell again, and, indeed, had made a good friend.

The Eucharist is celebrated in the form of a sacred meal where Christians gather to be nourished and enlivened by Jesus who once said, "I am the bread of life" (John 6:48). It is a meal where the Christ enters his followers as food, fills them with new life and bonds them more closely with each other and the people of the world.

Of Bread and Sacrifice

The Eucharist is also sacrificial in that the risen Lord makes present once again the earlier offering of love and compassion that he showed on Calvary. Our own sacrifices are joined with his and are accepted by the Creator. Parents, who sacrifice much to raise their youngsters, come to the altar. Workers, who give of themselves in factories, bring their offerings. Teachers, who devote so much time and energy to their students, come forth with their offerings. Boys and girls, who help their siblings, come to the altar. And the elderly, who counsel their neighbors and offer wisdom to children, step forth with their gifts. At liturgy, all of this is offered to the Creator through Jesus the Christ.

Elie Wiesel, the Jewish writer who survived the death camps of the Holocaust, tells a magnificent story of bread and sacrifice. Every day the guard would give the prisoners their one meal of the day—one piece of bread and some soup. Wiesel remembers so vividly how his father would break off half of his bread each day and give it to his small son. This little extra bread kept Elie alive, but his father grew weaker every day and eventually died.

Only later did Wiesel come to realize that his father, by sharing his bread, had hastened his own death. He now sees those pieces of bread as sacrificial bread which, for his young life, was the bread of life. Such is the Eucharist: bread that sacramentally symbolizes and makes present Jesus' death for us and his offer of new life.

Thanksgiving

The word *eucharist* actually means *thanksgiving*. At eucharistic liturgy, we give thanks to our Creator for all the gifts received. At the same time, those of us who are more fortunate are called to remember the millions who have never heard the Good News of God's love as well as those who are hungry and lack the comforts of home, clean water and proper health care. Since the Eucharist is a communion with the Lord and with each other, it invites us to share in his compassion for outcasts and the impoverished. It beckons us to share in his mission of service, in his commitment to justice.

The eucharistic liturgy is a time to thank God for the earth, all that lives on it and its vast resources. At the same time, it should awaken us to the degradation that is being inflicted on our environment and remind us that the earth is the Lord's, that we are held responsible to care for it and pass it on to future generations in healthy condition.

Finally, Eucharist is a time to remember all that God has done for us and to anticipate the kingdom that is to come. It is an opportunity to prepare for eternal life, pray for those who have gone before us and look with anticipation toward the time when we can join them at the Lord's heavenly table.

For Reflection

- *For Catholic Christians, the Eucharist is the central sacrament of the Church. Why do you think this is so? Is the Eucharist the central sacrament to you? If not, why not?*

- *How would you explain to a non-Catholic friend the Catholic belief in the Real Presence of Jesus in the Eucharist?*

- *Jesus spent much time at meals doing "table ministry." When have you witnessed "table ministry"?*

- *To this day, one says* Eucharisto *in Greek to thank someone. Do you think "Thank You" is an appropriate name for the Eucharist? Why or why not? What word would you choose to refer to the Eucharist?*

CHAPTER FOURTEEN

The Second Coming
of Jesus

It was on a hot, muggy day in Israel that our bus made its way along the Carmel Range and headed for Megiddo. Many scholars think that Megiddo is Armageddon, the place where the Book of Revelation says that the kings of the earth will assemble for a final battle before the end of the world (Revelation 16:16). Today nothing much is there other than a large mass of earth under which archaeologists have found twenty cities piled one on the other. Over thousands of years each of these glorious cities flourished as part of such powerful kingdoms as Canaan, Egypt, Israel, Babylon and Persia. One after the other, these magnificent kingdoms were destroyed, and Megiddo now stands as a symbol of how fleeting are power and wealth.

As we stood amidst the rubble of palaces and temples built millennia ago, we reflected on Jesus' second coming and remembered his words: "If any want to become my followers, let them deny themselves and take up their cross and follow me. For those who want to save their life will lose it, and those who lose their life for my sake will find it. For what will it profit them if they gain the whole world but forfeit their life? Or what will they give in return for their life? For the Son of Man is to come with his angels in the glory of his Father, and then he will repay everyone for what has been done" (Matthew 16:24-27). When Jesus comes, whether it be at our death or at the endtime when the Creator's plan has come to completion, those who lovingly gave themselves will enjoy eternal life.

Jesus and the Endtime

In the Gospels, Jesus taught with great passion about the endtime. As a Jew, he knew of the apocalyptic literature of his people. The word *apocalypse* means *revelation*. Some of the ancient Hebrew prophets revealed to their people in times of chaos and crisis that their God would come and defeat the powers of evil and restore the glory of his people Israel. The revelations were always highly allegorical and used images of catastrophe and dramatic "signs" that the fulfillment of God's kingdom was coming. The Book of Daniel and chapters in the prophetic books of Isaiah (13;24;25;26;27) and Ezekiel (32;38;39) are good examples of this type of literature.

In Mark's Gospel, Jesus spoke of what for a Jew would be one of the worst catastrophes possible—the destruction of the Temple (see Mark 13). Then Jesus continued, using the Jewish apocalyptic tradition and indicating the "signs" that would anticipate such a horrible event: false teachers, wars, rumors of wars, earthquakes and famines. The chaos is further imaged in terms of persecution of disciples and divisions among families.

Jesus warned his followers to flee such chaos and continue to be on guard against false messiahs. He told them of additional cosmic signs wherein the sun and moon would be darkened, stars would fall from the sky, the powers in heaven would shake and, finally, the messiah would come. In Mark's account, Jesus uses majestic language: "Then they will see 'the Son of Man coming in the clouds' with great power and glory. Then he will send out the angels, and gather his elect from the four winds, from the ends of the earth to the ends of heaven" (Mark 13:26-27). Jesus indicated that all this would come to pass soon (before the present generation passes away). Yet Jesus was emphatic that only the Father knew the day or hour of the endtime.

In the tradition of the great prophets, Jesus warned his disciples to prepare for this final time. He taught them to "be alert at all times" (Luke 21:36), to put their houses in order, to watch and stay fully awake. In Luke's gospel account, Jesus told his followers also to avoid self-indulgence, drunkenness and the anxiety of daily life.

Approaching Apocalyptic Writing

What are we to make of these apocalyptic teachings of Jesus, especially at this time when some commentators use them to predict the end of the world? For me, it is valuable to consult with biblical scholars. They understand the background and meaning of Scripture and can safeguard us from the frightening and even bizarre interpretations of apocalyptic writing that we heard in the days approaching the end of the second millennium.

Scholars tell us that the Gospels are multilayered. They contain (1) his followers' memories of Jesus' teaching, (2) the oral and written traditions that developed after his death and resurrection and (3) the concerns and insights of the early Christian communities that composed the various Gospels. If we apply this multilayered approach to the gospel accounts of the endtime, we first of all discover his disciples' memories of Jesus using the Jewish apocalyptic tradition to warn his people of the catastrophes they will bring upon themselves if they are unfaithful to their God. Jesus came to save his people from their sins, and he often grieves over the stubbornness and hardness of heart of so many of them. He condemns their hypocrisy, self-righteousness and exclusion of outcasts and little ones.

Jesus usually mixes his condemnation of evil with compassion and tenderness. Recall the touching story of the afternoon when he sat on the hillside overlooking his beloved Jerusalem and wept at the destruction that evil would bring to its people. He lamented, "If you, even you, had only recognized on this day the things that make for peace! But now they are hidden from your eyes" (Luke 19:42). On another occasion he cried out, "Jerusalem, Jerusalem, the city that kills the prophets and stones those who are sent to it! How often have I desired to gather your children together as a hen gathers her brood under her wings, and you were not willing" (Luke 13:34).

On another level, the gospel stories of the endtime reflect concerns of the first Christian communities. Early on, it seems the disciples anticipated that the second coming of Jesus was imminent. The Acts of the Apostles tells a story of Jesus' ascension where two men in white robes say, "Men of Galilee, why do you stand looking up toward heaven? This Jesus, who has been taken from you into heaven, will come in the same way as you saw him go to heaven" (Acts 1:11). And Paul the apostle anticipated the Lord's coming when he wrote to the community at Philippi: "But our citizenship is in heaven, and it is from there that we are expecting a Savior, the Lord Jesus Christ" (Philippians 3:20). The very early disciples, then, lived with intense anticipation of Jesus' coming again.

Shift in Focus, Meaning

As a whole generation of disciples did in fact pass away, Christians began to realize that Jesus' second coming would not likely happen soon. So, rather than preoccupying themselves with preparing for the endtime, they now shifted their attention to "getting on" with the business of spreading the gospel, establishing Church communities and dealing with the day-to-day struggles of life. The disciples still followed Jesus' admonitions to stay alert, be loving and caring in fulfilling their daily responsibilities, avoid sinful indulgence and be dedicated to prayer. But now their prayer, *"Maranatha"* ("Lord, come again"), was more a prayer that his Spirit would come to them in their everyday world, in people, the Word, the Eucharist and many other ways.

The endtime came to mean not only the end of the world but also of one's life. The disciples focused on their own "endtime" in death, praying that the Lord would come and take them into eternal life. Paul writes to the Corinthians, "So if anyone is in Christ, there is a new creation" (2 Corinthians 5:17). Yet the disciples still believed that the Lord would come again to all his people collectively when God's plan was completed. Paul tells the Ephesians that ultimately Christ will "gather up all things in him, things in heaven and things on earth" (Ephesians 1:10).

The disciples, of course, continued to experience the

catastrophes of life. As Christians they experienced rejection, persecution, even martyrdom. Yet, they knew from the apocalyptic teachings of Jesus that he would help them endure and defeat the powers of evil. He had promised them, "I am with you always, to the end of the age" (Matthew 28:20). His Spirit would be ever with them, and would uniquely come again when God's plan of salvation was complete.

The Book of Revelation addressed early Christians in this same Jewish-Christian apocalyptic tradition. Written by several authors near the end of the first century, it warned some of the Churches of Asia against being corrupted by the Roman religion and forbade them to give religious homage to the emperors. In the vivid allegorical imagery of apocalyptic literature, the Book of Revelation described the persecution of Christians by the beast (the Roman emperor) and dramatized how Jesus Christ would defeat Satan and reign as the savior. This highly poetic Christian book is, therefore, not so much concerned with predicting the end of the world as it is teaching that disciples must be faithful to the Lord, who will be with them all days and save them from evil.

The Apocalypse, the New Millennium

The apocalyptic tradition is especially relevant as we enter a new millennium. This is not a time to fear the coming of a wrathful God in a cataclysmic destruction of the world. It is an occasion to look forward in hope for new beginnings, and to have faith in the power of the Lord's Spirit in our personal lives and in our world. The apocalypse is a revelation that Jesus continues, again and again, to show his presence: to a young mother in agony over a miscarriage, to a husband who has lost his wife, to a soldier whose buddy lies dying in a jungle, to an AIDS patient in despair.

We are all aware that chaos and catastrophes always surround us. Personal tragedies and setbacks are part of the human situation. The dangers of nuclear, chemical, biological or environmental destruction are ever present. But as disciples of Jesus, we believe that his Spirit is with us and that he empowers us to overcome these evils. We believe that ultimately goodness and love cannot be defeated in our world, because Jesus is the Christ of the cosmos. Paul made this clear to the Church at Colossae when he wrote, "He is the image of the invisible God, the firstborn of all creation...All things have been created in him and for him. He himself is before all things and in him all things hold together" (Colossians 1:15-17). Theologian Karl Rahner declared that Jesus is "the heart of the cosmos," a savior ever with his people, moving the world to its fulfillment.

And so we watch—alert to the good, wary of evil. We protect ourselves, our children, parents, students and all those for whom we are responsible, from abuse, violence and oppression. We put our houses in order as we try to live decent lives and be disciples of Jesus who are loving, forgiving and concerned for peace and justice. And we pray, "Our Father...thy kingdom come"; "Hail Mary...pray for us sinners now and at the hour of our death"; "Lord, come again!"

For Reflection

- *Many fundamentalists, who interpret Scripture literally, read the Book of Revelation as sort of a secret code book that predicts specific events concerning the end of the world. Yet Jesus himself said that only the Father knows the day and the hour of the endtime. Why do you read the Book of Revelation?*

- *What did Jesus tell his followers to do about the end of the world?*

- *Read or retell in your own words the parable of the Ten Bridesmaids (Matthew 25:1-13). What does this parable say to you about dealing with the end of the world and Jesus' return?*

- *Imagine that a friend of yours, very upset after listening to a televangelist preach on the coming of the end of the world, comes to you for advice and insight about Jesus' second coming. What would you say to your friend?*

CHAPTER FIFTEEN

Jesus and the Spirit

A s the summer of 1997 ended, the world mourned the death of Mother Teresa of Calcutta, a woman who even during her life was proclaimed a saint. Perhaps more than any person in our time, she demonstrated by word and action the true meaning of the Spirit. She had a gift for experiencing the Spirit of Jesus in all people, and most especially in the poorest of the poor, the rejected, the outcast of society.

It is said that Mother Teresa heard her calling to leave her comfortable convent school and live the rest of her life in the slums of Calcutta when she encountered a dying man in the gutters of the city. She brought the man, who was covered with human waste and worms, to a place of safety, washed him, fed him and cared for him until he died. He told her that he had lived like an animal in the streets and that now he could die knowing that he was loved. Mother Teresa said she could never forget the smile of happiness on his face as he went to the Lord. She spent the rest of her life recognizing the presence of Jesus in everyone for whom she cared. We admire and revere Mother Teresa because she experienced so vividly what all of us Christians search for, the Spirit of Jesus.

The Spirit of God

All discussion of the Spirit begins with the Mystery we call God. Our Native American brothers and sisters referred to God as the Great Spirit. Likewise, our spiritual forebears, the Jews, viewed their Creator as a powerful Spirit who was the source, sustainer and goal of all the universe. The Hebrew word *ruah* means *wind* or *breath*, and it is used also to describe the Spirit of

God. In the magnificent story of creation in Genesis, the Spirit hovered over a formless and dark chaos and brought forth creation with a mere word (Genesis 1:1-6).

It is this same Spirit of God who led the chosen people from slavery in Egypt, and who gave the Law to Moses on Sinai. The Spirit of God repeatedly brought healing and forgiveness to the Hebrews, calling them back from their sinful ways to the covenant. The Spirit also "inspired" the prophets to confront those who bring injustice and oppression to God's children. The Psalmist prays, deeply aware of the need for this Spirit: "Do not cast me away from your presence, and do not take your holy spirit from me" (Psalm 51:11).

Life in the Spirit

The Gospels clearly reflect the early Christian belief that Jesus' entire life was Spirit-filled. The Gospel of Luke describes the annunciation of Jesus' birth as a coming of the Spirit. When Mary hears that she is to bear a child, she questions the angel as to how this can be because she is a virgin. The angel's answer echoes the creation story in Genesis: "The Holy Spirit will come upon you, and the power of the Most High will overshadow you; therefore the child to be born will be holy; he will be called Son of God" (Luke 1:35). In Mary's womb a new creation takes place. The Spirit who hovered over the chaos of the world to bring forth new life and goodness brings the world a savior. In this the new creation the creative Word of God becomes flesh and the Son of God comes to the world. The Gospel of Matthew puts it all succinctly: "She was found to be with child from the Holy Spirit" (Matthew 1:18).

As a child, Jesus would have been taught the Jewish reverence for the Spirit of God by Mary and Joseph. As a toddler, he no doubt saw his parents in prayer at home and at synagogue. Surely he often witnessed their deep intimacy with the Spirit. As Jesus grew up, he, more than any person who ever lived, experienced a oneness with the divine Spirit. At the very core of his being, he knew a unity with God that would ultimately pull him from his home and trade and lead him to be a healer and preacher. The purpose of his mission would be clearly expressed in his prayer the night before he died: "Holy Father, protect them in your name that you have given me, so that they may be one as we are one" (John 17:11b).

The Spirit Calls Jesus to Ministry .

The Gospels clearly reveal that Jesus' ministry reflected the power of the Spirit. At Jesus' baptism, the Holy Spirit descended upon him and the Father warmly spoke from above: "You are my Son, the Beloved; with you I am well pleased" (Luke 3:22). Then Jesus was led by the Spirit into the wilderness to be tested. And once Jesus had faced and resisted the powers of evil, he returned to Galilee filled with the Spirit and began his preaching in the synagogues.

On one occasion he showed up in his own hometown and read from Isaiah in the synagogue: "The Spirit of the Lord is upon me, because he has anointed me to bring good news to the poor" (Luke 4:18). When Jesus identified himself with the message in the reading, his neighbors were at first impressed. But when he began to imply that he was actually a prophet and that they would reject him, they drove him out of town and even tried to kill him. From then on Jesus would have to move on and do his work in Capernaum and other areas of Galilee. Preaching about the power of the Spirit, and, indeed, embodying the Spirit in his life would be dangerous for Jesus and ultimately would bring on his execution.

Jesus was at times accused by his enemies of being a charlatan who cured through the power of Satan. Nothing upset Jesus more, for he knew that the power that went through his hands as he touched diseased or disabled persons and healed them was the tender loving power of the Spirit. Jesus could see the love and joy in those who were made whole through the power and presence of the Creator. He knew that such peace and happiness could not be brought about through the power of Satan. On one occasion Jesus made this very clear to the Pharisees who were accusing him of consorting with evil powers. Jesus told them that his work was "by the Spirit of

God," and he insisted that his miracles were authentic signs that the kingdom of God was indeed in their midst (Matthew 12:28). The kingdom of God, or the loving, saving presence of God in the world was at the center of Jesus' message. And he knew full well that only the work of the Spirit could bring this kingdom to fulfillment.

A Promise Made and Kept

On the night before he died, Jesus promised his followers that he would send the Spirit to them. Jesus promised that this Spirit of truth would be with them always to help them, guide them and give them the strength and courage they needed to give witness to him (John 16). After Jesus was raised from the dead, he kept that promise as he returned to his followers in their confusion and fear to bring them peace and forgiveness. How privileged were these early disciples to experience Jesus in such glory and to hear his simple invitation, "Receive the Holy Spirit" (John 20:22).

It was on the Jewish feast of Pentecost that everything seemed to come clear for the apostles as they gathered with Mary and other members of Jesus' family. Suddenly, there was the sound of wind (*ruah*) and the flashes of fire as "all of them were filled with the Holy Spirit..." (Acts 2:4). Peter spoke to the masses, urging them to be baptized in the name of Jesus Christ so that their sins would be forgiven and they, too, could receive the holy Spirit (Acts 2:38). The Church of Jesus Christ was born that day, and from then on all Christians would identify the Spirit of God with the Spirit of Jesus. Paul would make this clear to the Church in Corinth when he taught that when we learn from the Spirit "we have the mind of Christ" (1 Corinthians 2:16b).

The Age of the Spirit

In this century, Christians have awakened to the presence of the Spirit in their lives. Too often in the past the notion of the Spirit was limited to the image of a mysterious dove or to the sacrament of Confirmation. The Second Vatican Council, the most significant event in our Church in this century, seems to have given Jesus' disciples today a new awareness of the power of the Spirit in the Church and throughout the entire world. The saintly Pope John XXIII wanted the council to be a new Pentecost, and indeed it was.

In many ways the Church was reborn in the Spirit and was filled with freshness and new life. The Church was returned in new ways to all the people of God, Jesus was placed at the center, the Scriptures were restored as a prime resource, and the celebration of the sacraments were all renewed. The Spirit of Jesus also led the Church to take its place in the world as a defender of the oppressed and the poor. And Christ opened the minds and hearts of Catholics to other Churches and religions. Most recently this renewal in the Spirit was displayed for the world in 1997, when a million young people from one hundred and sixty countries gathered outside Paris to celebrate Eucharist with John Paul II. The pope, standing before a multinational crowd similar to that which Peter faced on the first Pentecost, reminded the young people of the Spirit's presence in their midst and told them, "Your journey does not end here. Continue to contemplate God's glory and God's love and you will receive the enlightenment needed to build the civilization of love, to help our brothers and sisters to see the world transfigured by eternal wisdom and love."

Two Women and the Spirit

In addition to Mother Teresa, another outstanding woman, Diana, Princess of Wales, died in the summer of 1997. In many ways their lives could not have been more different. Diana represented nobility, wealth, glamour and fashion. Mother Teresa was a woman whose life stood for simplicity, poverty and complete self-sacrifice. Diana seems to have been deeply influenced by the saintly Mother Teresa and her compassion for the poor. The world was shocked and deeply anguished over the loss of both women, in part because they had both reached out to the poor and outcasts of the world.

The Spirit of the Lord uniquely touched the lives of these two very different women, and even on several occasions brought them together to witness to his gospel message: "Truly I tell you, just as you did it to one of the least of these who are members of my family, you did it to me" (Matthew 25:40). As each of these women was honored, the poor and outcasts of the world whom they had served were given center stage. And through this unlikely pair, a princess and a nun, the Spirit of the Lord somehow continued to renew the face of the earth.

The movements of the Spirit are unpredictable. As the Lord said, "The wind blows where it chooses, and you hear the sound of it, but you do not know where it comes from or where it goes. So it is with everyone who is born of the Spirit" (John 3:8). That same Spirit calls you and me to touch the lives of those about us with the presence and power of Jesus.

For Reflection

- *The Holy Spirit is often called the forgotten person of the Blessed Trinity. Why? How do you think of the Holy Spirit?*

- *Christians first receive the Holy Spirit in Baptism. They also receive the Spirit in the other sacraments, especially in Confirmation. What does the Holy Spirit bring to a Christian's life? to your life?*

- *When has the Holy Spirit been present in your life? How did you recognize the Holy Spirit?*

CHAPTER SIXTEEN

Jesus and His Church

W hen our three-year-old neighbor, Bobby, comes over to visit on our porch, my wife and I are always struck by the beauty and innocence of his face. When he looks up at us and tells us of his day at nursery school, his eyes shine with joy and his face is filled with trust and goodness. It is that same joy and peace that Pope John XXIII wanted to restore in Jesus' Church. When the saintly pontiff called for the Second Vatican Council in 1958, he used the image of a child's face and said that he wanted "to restore the simple and pure lines that the face of the Church of Jesus had at its birth."

John XXIII was too much a Church historian to idealize the early Christian communities and see them as gatherings of perfect saints. He knew that from the beginning the Churches had their share of sinful leaders and members. He realized that there were divisions and conflicts over such issues as circumcision, kosher food, divorce, sexual ethics, the humanity of Jesus and the time of the second coming. Nevertheless, Pope John believed that the Church had received from Jesus an essential unity and holiness that had to be constantly renewed. So he set out to restore the original vision of the Church where Jesus Christ was the center, and where communities of disciples faithfully dedicated themselves to the promotion of the kingdom of God.

Jesus at the Center

Jesus laid the foundations of the Church and has always been present as the center of the Church. The earliest communities were apostles and disciples who had accepted the invitation of this young carpenter from Galilee to change their lives and follow him. They were women and men who had walked the hillsides listening to his amazing teachings about the Abba God who created and sustained all things on earth. They had seen Jesus take little children on his lap to hug them and teach them about the love and care of God.

Many of the disciples had been present when Jesus quietly reached out to a blind person, a person with leprosy, or one who was disabled to restore that person to good health and happiness. Some had watched him change people caught up in evil ways into faithful followers now willing to share their wealth with the poor. A few had been there when Jesus was led off to be beaten, humiliated and crucified naked outside the city. Many had been privileged to experience Jesus after he had been raised from the dead.

These early disciples had come to recognize that Jesus was the Christ, their Lord and Savior. In the early community at Colossae, this faith in Jesus was proclaimed as follows: "He is the image of the invisible God, the firstborn of all creation; for in him all things in heaven and on earth were created, things visible and invisible, whether thrones or dominions or rulers or powers—all things have been created through him and for him. He himself is before all things, and in him all things hold together. He is the head of the body, the church; he is the beginning, the firstborn from the dead, so that he might come to have first place in everything" (Colossians 1:15-18).

Jesus had promised to be with his followers forever. He said, "And remember, I am with you always, to the end of the age" (Matthew 28:20). To this day Jesus has kept his word. His presence can be vividly experienced in the Scriptures, in the sacraments, in communities of faith, in people's lives, in events across the globe.

The Presence of Jesus

Jesus is present in inner-city soup kitchens, at village wells in Africa where mothers gather to fetch water for their families, and in the lives of migrant workers bending over in the hot sun to pick vegetables. He is within the hearts of prison administrators who will not permit inmates to be degraded or abused. From Rome to Tokyo, from Bosnia to Guatemala, Christ must be the center if the Church wishes to maintain its authenticity.

One of the major contributions of the Second Vatican Council was its proclamation that the Church is, first and foremost, people—the people of God. The council reminded all the Church that, though there are supporting and important institutional structures, official positions, titles, laws and traditions, the people are of primary importance. Church leaders were reminded that they were called to serve people rather than rule over them. Essentially, Church is about people of all nations, colors, races, genders and ages gathered in equality before the Lord Jesus Christ.

Paul expressed this when he wrote to the community in Galatia: "For in Christ Jesus you are all children of God through faith. As many of you as were baptized into Christ have clothed yourselves with Christ. There is no longer Jew or Greek, there is no longer slave or free, there is no longer male and female; for all of you are one in Christ Jesus" (Galatians 3:26-28). The author of the First Letter of Peter reminded another early Christian community what discipleship meant when he wrote: "You are a chosen race, a royal priesthood, a holy nation, God's own people" (1 Peter 2:9).

Authentic Christian communities are open and inclusive. There is, then, no place for prejudice or discrimination in our communities regarding a person's color, ethnic background, physical condition, gender, or sexual orientation. Our communities are true to the gospel if they are welcoming, affirming and nourishing toward all who come in his name. One of Jesus' most persistent teachings was that there were to be no outcasts, no untouchables. His healing touch and open arms were available to tiny and powerless children, to crooked tax collectors, hypocritical scribes, lepers, adulterers and prostitutes. Jesus offered forgiveness to the rich, the poor, the saintly and the sinful and welcomed them as children whom the Abba God loved unconditionally. Our Christian communities can be no different.

Today Christian communities come in all shapes and sizes. There are tiny storefront gospel groups where people gather to share fellowship and praise the Lord. There are magnificent cathedrals where throngs of disciples come together to celebrate Mass. In towns and cities throughout the world there are parishes where people gather to baptize new members, seek forgiveness of their sins, gain healing for their afflictions and celebrate Eucharist together. Throughout the Third World, there are base communities, where people who are oppressed come together to pray to the Lord for liberation. In many parishes, small faith communities gather for prayer, support and spiritual nourishment. There are families—domestic churches—where members share their lives, their meals and their problems with gospel love and care.

The synoptic Gospels (Matthew, Mark and Luke) mention the kingdom of God more than a hundred times. It is clear that Jesus' teachings about the kingdom of God are central to his message and key to understanding the nature of the Church. In Mark's Gospel, the earliest one, Jesus begins his public mission with the words, "The time is fulfilled, and the kingdom of God has come near; repent, and believe in the good news" (Mark 1:15).

Promoting the Kingdom

The notion of the kingdom of God was not original with Jesus, although he did give it a newness in light of his unique experience of God as Abba. The Hebrews during the time of the monarchy used the image of "king" for their God because they saw Yahweh to be the all-powerful creator who guided, protected and liberated them. The kingdom of God was indeed the very being of God, the presence of the divine in the world. The kingdom of God might be described as the powerful, loving and saving presence of God, a presence that is revealed in the daily lives of faithful people.

God's reign was interpreted differently by the Jewish teachers in Jesus' day. Some saw it as a reign of terror and judgment which punished pagans and sinners. Many of Jesus' fellow Jews had been taught that their physical afflictions were a punishment from God. Others saw God's reign as distant and remote, one which left humans confused and even in despair. When Jesus began to teach, he soon realized that some had forgotten the loving, forgiving, caring Yahweh of their Scriptures.

Jesus took an extraordinary stand in his teaching about the kingdom of God. He said that the kingdom was near at hand; that the presence of Abba was as near as the wind, as bountiful as the harvest or a full catch of fish, and as warm and bright as the sunshine. Jesus saw the presence of the kingdom in the beauty and fragrance of lilies, in the busyness of birds feeding, and in the trusting embrace of a child. For Jesus, the kingdom, or "reign," of God was not to be found in violence, oppression or the abuse of power. Rather it was to be found in love, gentleness, humility and self-sacrifice. God's power was described by Jesus as "blessedness" or "holiness," and he said it could be recognized in people who were poor in spirit, meek, merciful and clean of heart. Blessedness could be found in the hearts of those who mourned for others or who had a hunger for righteousness; in peacemakers, and in those who suffered persecution (Matthew 5:3-10).

The kingdom of God and the Church are closely related. The Church is a people, a community struggling to be faithful disciples of Jesus. The Church, therefore, must constantly strive to recognize the powerful presence of God's kingdom in its midst. The Church needs to stand as a sign of the love, forgiveness and blessedness of God's kingdom. It is called to promote, preach and give example of the loving power of Jesus and his kingdom.

The power of the kingdom is not a power for domination, control or abuse. Rather, the people of the Church are empowered by the Spirit to serve, to sacrifice, to be there for those in need. Divine power is a loving force that seeks justice, reaches out to the oppressed and brings comfort to the needy.

The Power of Service

The power that drives the kingdom of God is love. One early disciple of Jesus equated love with God and saw Jesus as the perfect expression of this love. He wrote, "Beloved, let us love one another, because love is from God; everyone who loves is born of God and knows God. Whoever does not love does not know God, for God is love. God's love was revealed among us in this way: God sent his only Son into the world so that we might live through him" (1 John 4:7-9).

It is said that the kingdom of God is both "already" and "not yet." The presence of Jesus Christ is always at hand in his Church, teaching, healing, forgiving, guiding. Yet the Church is ever "on the way," moving toward a time of ultimate fulfillment. As we enter a new millennium, we can see two thousand years of the Church's history behind us. At the same time, we look toward a vast uncharted future where countless disciples will continue to promote the kingdom of God. Our time for such a mission is now.

For Reflection

- *Pope John XXIII was elected as an interim pope by the cardinals in the 1958 conclave. He was elderly and not in the best of health at the time of his election. Only three months after his election as pope, John XXIII surprised everyone when he announced that he was convening a general council of the Church. In his announcement, he called for an updating (aggiornamento) of the Church, an opening of the Church's windows to the Holy Spirit and a new Pentecost for the Church. In what ways has Pope John's purposes for the Second Vatican Council been realized? What work from Vatican II do you think still needs to be done?*

- *Why do we need a Church? What purpose or purposes does a Church serve?*

- *An early commentator on the Scriptures saw the Church in the character of the innkeeper in the parable of the Good Samaritan. What about the innkeeper image is like the Church? What image would you use for the Church?*

- *Jesus said that the Church would endure until the end of time. The Church has had its ups and downs through the centuries. What strengths do you see in the Church of the first two thousand years? What weaknesses? What would you like the Church to be in the third millennium?*

BIBLIOGRAPHY

Boff, Leonardo. Ecology and Liberation. Maryknoll, N.Y.: Orbis, 1995.

___. *Jesus Christ Liberator*. Maryknoll, N.Y.: Orbis, 1978.

Brown, Raymond F. *The Churches the Apostles Left Behind*. Mahwah, N.J.: Paulist Press, 1984.

Castelli, Jim (ed.). *How I Pray*. New York: Ballantine Books, 1994.

Collins, Gerald, S.J. *Experiencing Jesus*. Mahwah, N.J.: Paulist Press, 1995.

Cwiekowski, Francis. *The Beginnings of the Church*. Mahwah, N.J.: Paulist Press, 1988.

Dorr, Donal. *The Social Justice Agenda*. Maryknoll, N.Y.: Orbis, 1991.

Edwards, Denis. *Jesus the Wisdom of God*. Maryknoll, N.Y.: Orbis, 1995.

Harrington, Wilfrid J. *Revelation*. Collegeville, Minn.: Liturgical Press, 1993.

Hellwig, Monika. *The Eucharist and the Hunger of the World*. Kansas City, Mo.: Sheed & Ward, 1992.

Hill, Brennan R. *Christian Faith and the Environment*. Maryknoll, N.Y.: Orbis, 1988.

John Paul II, edited by Paul Thigpen. *Celebrate 2000: A Three-Year Reader (Reflections on Jesus, the Holy Spirit and the Father)*. Ann Arbor, Mich.: Servant Publications, 1996.

John Paul II. *Tertio Millennio Adveniente (As the Third Millennium Draws Near)*. Boston: Pauline Books & Media, 1994.

Johnson, Elizabeth A. *Consider Jesus*. New York: Crossroad, 1992.

Johnson, Elizabeth, C.S.J. *Women, Earth and Creator Spirit*, Mahwah, N.J.: Paulist Press, 1993.

King, Ursula. *Christ in All Things.* Maryknoll, N.Y.: Orbis, 1997.

Macy, Gary. *The Banquet's Wisdom.* Mahwah, N.J.: Paulist Press, 1992.

The Many Faces of Jesus: Matthew 25 Series (four videocassettes; sold separately). Dubuque, Iowa: Brown-Roa Publishing Media, 1993.

Moltmann-Wendel, Elizabeth. *The Women Around Jesus.* New York: Crossroad, 1982.

Perkins, Pheme. *The Book of Revelation.* Collegeville, Minn.: Liturgical Press, 1985.

Saldarini, Anthony. *Matthew's Christian-Jewish Community.* Chicago: University of Chicago Press, 1994.

Sanders, E. P. *Jesus and Judaism.* Philadelphia: Fortress, 1987.

Schneiders, Sandra. *Women and the Word.* Mahwah, N.J.: Paulist Press, 1986.

Senior, Donald. *Jesus, a Gospel Portrait.* Mahwah, N.J.: Paulist Press, 1992.

Sloyan, Gerard. *Jesus in Focus.* Mystic, Conn.: Twenty-Third Publications, 1994.

Upton, Julia. *A Church for the Next Generation: Sacraments in Transition.* Collegeville, Minn.: Liturgical Press, 1990.

Vermes, Geza. *Jesus the Jew.* Philadelphia: Fortress, 1981.

Vest, Norvene. *No Moment Too Small: Rhythms of Silence, Prayer and Holy Reading.* Kalamazoo, Mich.: Cistercian Publications/Cowley Publications, 1994.

Witherington, Ben. *Women in the Ministry of Jesus.* London: Cambridge University Press, 1988.

Zannoni, Arthur E. "Jesus as Prophet," *Catholic Update.* Cincinnati: St. Anthony Messenger Press, December 1994.

___. *Jesus of the Gospels: Teacher, Storyteller, Friend, Messiah.* Cincinnati: St. Anthony Messenger Press, 1996.